THE
HAMILTONIANS

Edited by
Margaret Houghton

James Lorimer & Company Ltd., Publishers
Toronto

Dedicated to all those who volunteer to preserve their local heritage, and particularly those from the historical societies who participated in writing the book: Ancaster Township Historical Society, Beverly Heritage Society, Dundas Valley Historical Society, Glanbrook Heritage Society, Head-of-the-Lake Historical Society, Stoney Creek Historical Society and Waterdown-East Flamborough Heritage Society.

James Lorimer & Company Ltd. acknowledges the support of the Ontario Arts Council. We acknowledge the financial support of the Government of Canada through the Book Publishing Industry Development Program (BPIDP) for our publishing activities. We acknowledge the support of the Government of Ontario through the Ontario Media Development Corporation's Ontario Book Initiative. We acknowledge the support of the Canada Council for the Arts for our publishing program.

ONTARIO ARTS COUNCIL
CONSEIL DES ARTS DE L'ONTARIO

The Canada Council | Le Conseil des Arts
for the Arts | du Canada

Visual sources:
All images provided by Special Collections, Hamilton Public Library except for those listed below: Dundas Valley Historical Society: 22, 123; Erland Lee Museum: 98; Farmer Family: 57, 58; Glanbrook Heritage Society, 19; Paul Kuzyk: 4; Waterdown-East Flamborough Heritage Society: 106, 116

National Library of Canada Cataloguing in Publication
Houghton, Margaret
      The Hamiltonians : 100 fascinating lives / Margaret Houghton.

Includes index.
ISBN 1-55028-804-0

      1. Hamilton (Ont.)—Biography. 2. Hamilton (Ont.)—History.
I. Title.
FC3098.25.H69 2003 971.3'52'0099   C2003-903621-9

James Lorimer & Company Ltd., Publishers
35 Britain Street
Toronto, ON M5A 1R7
www.lorimer.ca

Printed and bound in Canada

Gore Park, Hamilton, Canada.

INTRODUCTION

The story of any city is the story of the people who have lived there. The people who make a city exciting and unique are not necessarily the famous or well-known inhabitants, but the ordinary, everyday people who call that city home and give it a character and flavour that is unique to that city. All cities have a character that is unlike any other city and distinctive to itself and the people who live there. No two cities can ever be alike because of that. The mix of people that define a city is not predictable. What shapes the character of a city more than anything else is serendipity. Who chanced to come there and stay to shape its development is as variable as the wind.

Hamilton is no exception. From the earliest days of settlement in the 1780s right up to the present time, the story of Hamilton has been defined by the lives and experiences of the people who lived here. Some Hamiltonians were born here and spent their entire lives in the city without ever leaving it. To them, their city, with its limited parameters, was their world and they treasured it. They never sought the wider pastures that others did. Some Hamiltonians were born here but hungered for adventures outside the known and predictable. They left to explore exciting and different worlds outside the city. However, no matter where they went in the world they still carried their hometown with them as they made their mark. Still other Hamiltonians were adopted citizens who chose the city for their

home. Although they were not born here they were as proud of their chosen city as any other citizen. These immigrants brought a wealth of diverse experience to their adopted city and made their own unique contribution. It is the diversity of the life experiences of all of the citizens of Hamilton, past and present, that has made this community unique and individual. All of the people who have ever called Hamilton home have all made their mark in one way or another and have left an indelible legacy that defines the character of the city. That legacy and the story of the people who created it are the focus of *The Hamiltonians*.

Who were these people who lived here, who shaped the city that we live in today? What unique and special contribution did they make? Why are they remembered when so many others have been forgotten?

Who better to tell us than those people of the present city of Hamilton who study the history of our community? And what is history but simply the study of the people, who lived, loved, worked and played in our community?

Hamilton is blessed with a number of excellent historical societies whose members work hard to document the history of the communities that now make up the amalgamated city of Hamilton. They tell the stories of those who have gone before us. There are active historical societies in Ancaster, Beverly, Dundas, Flamborough, Glanbrook, Hamilton and Stoney Creek with members who were eager to join in the quest to define our city by the people who have lived here. This dedication to the study and preservation of the past is not new. It has always been a focus of many of the people who lived in Hamilton to preserve and document the history of our community.

There have been active historical societies in Hamilton dating back to the nineteenth century when the Wentworth Historical Society was formed to preserve and protect our historical legacy. Their members, from all levels of society, and from all areas of the original county of Wentworth, sought out stories from our past and preserved them in books and articles that are as vivid and colourful today as they were over 100 years ago. Some of the historians who documented our history are now history themselves with their own fascinating stories to tell (Gordon Allison and Clementina Fessenden).

To document the history of the people of this fascinating city, therefore, it seemed only appropriate to go to the people of the historical societies of today who work so diligently to keep our collective history alive and vital. Each historical society that participated in *The Hamiltonians* was asked to choose the people from their geographical area that they felt had interesting stories that should be told. The people chosen were to be either buried in the community or have a memorial dedicated to them. The contributors to *The Hamiltonians* did not try to tell the entire life story of these people. They have, instead, tried to highlight some interesting facets of the lives of these earlier citizens — to give a vignette that makes them come alive to the readers of today. Whatever their life history might have been, dramatic, sorrowful, or perfectly ordinary, something made them stand out from the rest for the historians who chose them. These Hamilton historians of today chose the famous and the infamous, the known and the unknown, the good, the bad and the somewhat questionable characters that have shaped the city of Hamilton and its surrounding communities. There are murderers (William Cooke and Michael McConnell) and murder victims (the Fields children, Ethel Kinrade and Bessie Perri); victims of natural disaster from the Desjardins Bridge Disaster (Great Western Railway crew) to the *Titanic* (Dr Alfred Pain); the only person in Hamilton's history who is documented as having been killed by a runaway cow (Captain Edward Zealand); politicians (Charles Goodenough Booker, Nora Frances Henderson, Sir John Gibson); eccentrics (Robert Kirkland Kernighan and David Chambers); victims of war (Mae Belle Sampson, Margaret Hayworth and the Royal Air Force Servicemen); philanthropists (Harriet Vaux Sanford and Matthew Hayes, who was also less than philanthropic with his chosen profession of bookie); educators (Martha Julia Cartmell, Elizabeth Ridler, George Washington Johnson and Susan Bennetto); scientists and inventors (Charles Field and Daniel Brand Marsh); heroic members of the police services killed in the line of duty (James Barron and Troy) as well as the only recipient of the Victoria Cross to be buried in Hamilton (John McGovern). There are also nurses, doctors, farmers, firemen, bootleggers, undertakers, manufacturers and even those forever nameless souls who died in the great cholera epidemics of the middle nineteenth century. They are all part of our history and have made Hamilton what it is today.

History is a living thing just as the people that make up our past were once living people. It evolves and changes as the people who make up our communities evolve and change. Today's Hamilton is as different from the Hamilton of a century ago as the Hamilton of a century from now will be different from today. But one thing will never change. Hamilton will be the city of its people. They define what it has been, what it is today and what it will become.

The Hamiltonians is, therefore, a celebration and a commemoration of all of them, the people of Hamilton and what they have contributed to the city they call home.

Stoney Creek Battlefield.

Monument to Soldiers who fell at Battle of Stoney Creek, 1813

STONEY CREEK, NEAR HAMILTON, ONT., CANADA.

Stoney Creek Village   108456

Fire Chief Aitchison races up James Street North in 1892.

ALEXANDER AITCHISON
(1849-1905)
Buried in Hamilton Cemetery, 777 York Boulevard, Section A9

The history of Hamilton's modern fire department dates from the beginning of 1879 with the appointment of Alexander Aitchison as Fire Chief. He had begun his career as a lantern bearer with the volunteer fire brigade. He radically reformed the department over many city councillors' strenuous objections.

In 1882 the Bay Street Station opened, and in June of that same year the first steam fire-engine was purchased. In 1885 the Victoria Avenue Station opened. Chief Aitchison introduced the first swinging harness and sliding pole in Canada. He changed the department over to an entirely paid organization and taught his firemen the importance of arriving at a fire as soon as possible after the alarm sounded. At one point they held the world's record for harnessing and leaving the engine house.

Alexander Wingfield, a local poet, wrote a verse to celebrate Hamilton's Fire Department.

Our Hamilton Fire Brigade
All honour to our "Fire Brigade"
The gallant and the brave;
"Aye ready!" are they in our need,
They always run to save.
By night or day they ne'er refuse
To lend their willing aid,
But do their duty manfully —
Our gallant "Fire Brigade"

The Hamilton Fire Department sometimes roamed a little farther afield than Hamilton. In 1904 Chief Aitchison, ten men, a steam pumper and a rig with 1,400 feet of hose and a couple of horses were loaded onto a special freight train and rushed off to Toronto to help fight the disastrous fire burning there. In return, Toronto sent the Hamilton Fire Department a beautiful illuminated certificate in thanks.

It was Chief Aitchison's stress on speed that led to the accident that took his life in 1905. He died of injuries suffered when his buggy collided with the chemical wagon at the corner of King and Hughson Streets and he was thrown against the base of the Sir John A. Macdonald statue. The fire the firefighters were rushing to was a simple grass fire set by boys playing with matches but that did not make any difference to the Chief. Every fire was important and speed was essential.

As a result of the Chief's accident the statue of Sir John A. Macdonald was moved from the middle of the intersection, turned to face east and relocated in Gore Park.

Margaret Houghton

GORDON ALLISON
(1918-1998)
Buried in North Glanford Cemetery, Highway #6, Glanbrook

Gordon Allison, pictured in 1936.

Traditionally, people's tombstones are located in cemeteries. Monuments to their lives' achievements may be found elsewhere: memorials in city squares, plaques in parks bearing their names, towns named in their honour. Gordon Allison's legacy may be found in Special Collections at Hamilton Public Library, the research section of the Hamilton Branch of the Ontario Genealogical Society (OGS) and the archives of the Glanbrook Heritage Society. For the last few years of his busy life, Gordon worked at home on a compilation of births, deaths and marriages as reported from 1846 to 1893 in the *Hamilton Spectator*. He was part-way through 1894 when he died on 3 February 1998 in his home at Ryckman's Corners, part of the farm that had been in the Allison family for 150 years.

To quote James Elliott in the *Spectator*: "He was many things — teacher, musician, quiltmaker, francophile, traveler and caregiver — but primarily he was a tireless researcher and archivist of early Hamilton history throughout his adult life."

Gordon went to public school in Glanford Township, attended high school in Caledonia and trained as a teacher at Hamilton Normal School. His early teaching career was in Amherstburg, before his return to Hamilton in 1953 where he spent 20 years in the English department of Delta Secondary School, Hamilton Board of Education.

In the late 1980s, Gordon bought a microfilm reader and dozens of films of the *Hamilton Spectator* from 1846 to 1908. He began his greatest legacy, transcribing the births, deaths and marriages in full detail into print on his trusty Underwood typewriter. Fully indexed copies were sent to Special Collections at the Hamilton Public Library free of charge. After his death, his own copies were distributed to the Hamilton Branch OGS. An extra set was then given to the Glanbrook Heritage Society, which now carries on his work.

Gordon's historical passion extended to research of dozens of early Hamilton Mountain families as well as a detailed history of Barton Stone United Church, its families and its ministers. Some of the material goes back to 1811: biographies containing photos where available, family histories and obituaries of those buried in Barton Stone cemetery. Many families received free copies of his research efforts simply because he wanted to share his passion for genealogy and family history.

Again quoting James Elliott: "His lawyer, Alec Beasley, says — 'I don't know what he couldn't do. He did about everything a woman or man could do.'"

Art French

THOMAS BAIN
(1834–1915)
Buried in Grove Cemetery, York Street, Dundas, Pineview Section

It was unanimous! Canadian history had been made. The new Speaker of the House of Commons had been nominated without any opposition from Sir Wilfrid Laurier's governing Liberals, or from Sir Charles Tupper's Conservatives.

Thomas Bain, Liberal Member of Parliament for Wentworth County

The Honourable Thomas Bain, Speaker of the House of Commons, in 1899.

since 1872 and Chairman of the Committee on Agriculture and Colonization, graciously and humbly accepted his new position in late summer of 1899. Noted for his crisp and concise speaking style, he made an acceptance speech that was the briefest on record.

His appointment to the Speaker's Chair established many firsts in Canadian history. Aside from being the first speaker elected unanimously by all members of parliament, he was the first and only farmer ever to hold the position. He was the first to serve only a partial term: he succeeded his predecessor, J.D. Edgar, upon his death in August 1899 until parliament was dissolved in October 1900. He then retired after 28 years of service on Parliament Hill.

The speakership is a position where respect is commanded from parliamentarians and outsiders alike. Mr Bain had a deserved reputation of being kind in nature and fair in spirit, and was widely respected by both political allies and opponents. In an office surrounded by pomp, ceremonies and procedures, Thomas Bain retained the common touch. He was an extremely shy, modest man and, being one of the most experienced and respected members of the House, was a perfect choice to preside over the final session of the eighth parliament.

Although unilingual, Mr Bain recognized the need for the French language to become more commonly used in parliament. As Speaker, he acknowledged the disadvantages of having a unilingual officer presiding over a bilingual assembly. He noted that, while most French members understood English, few English members understood French.

Upon his retirement from parliament, Thomas Bain was presented with the Speaker's Chair now on permanent display at the Dundas Historical Society Museum.

Following his political career, Thomas Bain served as president of two business enterprises until his death on 18 January 1915 at Bonnington, his Dundas home.

Stan Nowak

ABRAHAM BAKER
(1775-1838)
Buried in Rock Chapel United Church Cemetery, Rock Chapel Road,
West Flamborough Township

East Flamborough Township was among the last of the early surveyed townships to receive settlers, and it remained empty and isolated for over a decade. About 1803, a young American named Abraham Baker and his wife, Esther Yake, from Lancaster County, Pennsylvania came northwards hoping to settle and purchase property. The family had no connections to the British Crown during the American Revolutionary War, so they were like hundreds of other Americans who crossed the border into Upper Canada, uncertain and fearing that their religious faith or political convictions would be compromised by remaining in the new republic.

On arrival, the Bakers "squatted" on Lot 13, Concession 4, East Flamborough and began attempts to purchase the property. Abraham Baker made repeated applications to obtain ownership, but the requests met with no success, as did those of his friend, neighbour and fellow American, Jacob Long.

Early in 1812, both men submitted petitions to the Honourable Isaac Brock to lease their lands. Documents in the National Archives of Canada record Abraham Baker paying money to the Receiver General's Office for Crown Lot 13, Concession 4, and depositing a certificate stating that "he had resided in Upper Canada for upwards of eight years" and that during that time he "had behaved himself with great propriety, that he was sober, industrious and an honest man and deserved a grant of Crown Land."

On 17 March 1812, Abraham's petition was reviewed and referred to the

Executive Council of Upper Canada, where approval was recommended, "with rent to commence the next quarter day after the approval date." Just three months later, Upper Canada and the United States were at war, and whether deliberately — because of Abraham's nationality — or accidentally, the approval was never finalized. Unaware that he was still not entitled to be on the property, Abraham and his family, which now numbered six children, established a farm and constructed barns, outbuildings and a two-storey frame house.

On 3 January 1828, the Crown Patent for the property was granted to King's College, Toronto, so Abraham Baker had to begin again with requests. Not until 1831 was the deed to his property finally obtained, and that at the cost of £247 10s.

Abraham Baker died 12 November 1838. His small white tombstone is the earliest recorded interment still standing in the pioneer section of the cemetery.

Sylvia Wray

HUGH COSSART BAKER, JR
(1846-1931)
Buried in the Hamilton Cemetery, 777 York Boulevard,
Section Christ's Church Cathedral — A

Hamilton's first telephone exchange, the first in the British Empire and the second in North America, was created because of a chess game.

Hugh Cossart Baker, Jr was born to wealth and social prominence. His father, the first manager of the Bank of Montreal in Hamilton, founded Canada's first life insurance company, Canada Life, in 1847.

At the age of 19, Baker Jr enlisted in the 13th Battalion Volunteer Militia Infantry and carried the battalion's colours against the Fenians at Ridgeway, 1 June 1866. After military service, he followed in his father's footsteps and became a prominent citizen, banker and stockbroker. His entrepreneurial drive helped create the Hamilton Street Railway Company, the Hamilton Real Estate Association and the Canada Fire and Marine Insurance Company — all before he was 30 years old.

Baker's spare time was spent playing chess with his friends T.C. Mewburn and Charles D. Cory. To enable them to communicate their moves to one another in three separate residences, they had a telegraph wire strung between their homes and formed the West Side Domestic Telegraph Company. The line ran between Herkimer Street, Main Street West and Maiden Lane.

Hugh Cossart Baker, Jr., Hamilton's telephone pioneer.

When Baker learned of Alexander Graham Bell's invention, and then experienced the telephone in use at the Philadelphia International Exposition, he decided to test the communication tool in Hamilton. He leased four telephones, installed one in his own home and installed the others in the homes of his two chess partners and the home of Cory's sister. On 29 August 1877, the telephone replaced the telegraph as the means to discuss their chess moves. This was the first telephone transmission between more than two telephones, on one circuit, in Canada.

Baker was convinced that there was a commercial application for this technology. On 1 January 1878, he formed the Hamilton District Telegraph Company. Later that year he had the foresight to purchase exclusive rights to telephone installations in the counties of Wentworth, Halton and Haldimand. On 15 July 1878, Hamilton's first exchange opened. It was housed in cramped quarters at the corner of King and Hughson Streets, on the top floor of the Hamilton Provident and Loan building.

In 1880 the Hamilton Telephone Company, as it had come to be called, received a federal charter. It was this charter that enabled the creation of the

Bell Telephone Company of Canada. Hugh Cossart Baker, Jr was manager of the Ontario division until he retired in 1909.

Donna Reid & Robin McKee

GEORGE BAMBERGER
(1839-1908)
Buried in Hamilton Cemetery, 777 York Boulevard,
Section Christ's Church Cathedral — E

George Bamberger was "in the catbird seat" and he knew it. It was too good an opportunity to let pass and he was determined to take advantage of it. When Britton Bath Osler approached Bamberger, seeking permission to build his railway line through Bamberger's West Hamilton property, he saw it as a golden opportunity.

On 11 May 1875, Dundas lawyer B.B. Osler called a meeting of property owners George Bamberger, Joseph Cline, J.G. Binkley and R.R. Wardell at Bamberger's Half-Way House. The watering hole and traveller's rest for people travelling to Dundas had been in the family since George's grandfather, Samuel Bamberger, built it in 1824. In 1927 the Half-Way House was *The Half-Way* demolished. Three years later the Catholic School Board built Canadian *House in later* Martyrs School on the Main Street West site.

years, showing Osler proposed to build the Hamilton-to-Dundas horse-drawn railway *the roofed-over* through their properties, and Cline, Binkley and Wardell agreed to his pro- *platform beside* posal. George Bamberger did not. Knowing he was the last holdout put him *the tracks.* in a strong bargaining position. If Osler hoped to complete the building of

the railway he would have to meet Bamberger's demands. They did reach a leasing agreement. All trains would be required to make a mandatory five-minute stop at the Half-Way House. This stop would give tired and thirsty workers returning home from their day's labour time to enjoy a quick glass of beer.

To accommodate his patrons Bamberger built a roofed platform alongside the tracks with a covered walk to the door of his bar. When four of the five minutes of the stop had passed, the bartender was instructed to give a free glass of beer to the engineer and conductor. This stretched the short break to seven or eight minutes. The result was that Bamberger sold more beer to his thirsty patrons. The free enterprise system was alive and well!

Prior to the building of the rail line, many of the conductors were stage-coach drivers between Hamilton and Dundas. On 3 June 1879, the Hamilton and Dundas Street Railway officially opened with steam locomotives instead of horses. By 1900 the Hamilton Cataract Power Company bought the line and converted it to electricity. Because of increased competition from automobiles and buses, the Dummy, as the little train was affectionately known, made its last run on 5 September 1923.

Clare Crozier

CONSTABLE JAMES BARRON
(1856–1903)
Buried in Hamilton Cemetery, 777 York Boulevard, Section Q3

Constable James Barron, the first Hamilton police officer to be killed in the line of duty.

We tend to think of life 100 years ago as more idyllic, more gracious than today, that policemen of that era, big and brawny as they were, handled street crime with nothing more than physical strength and, from time to time, an accurately wielded truncheon.

While that may have been essentially true, Monday 24 October 1903 proved to be the exception to the rule. That was when Constable James Barron became the first Hamilton officer to be murdered on duty when a routine arrest went horribly wrong.

Around 1:00 a.m., Constable Barron said goodbye to Constable Hawkins, the desk officer at No. 3 Station on King William Street, before wandering at regulation pace down Catharine Street North towards the Gore (present-day Wilson Street).

When he reached the intersection of Catharine and the Gore, William Mills came out of his house and whistled to get his attention. Constable Barron listened intently as Mills told him about two suspicious men his mother had seen go towards the rear of the house next door, which was owned by the city solicitor William Mackelcan. Declining Mill's offer of assistance, the officer clambered over the fence and walked off into the darkness.

Once he was at the rear of the house, Constable Barron saw a man on a ladder trying to break in through a second floor window. What he did not see, however, was the second man concealed in dense shrubbery nearby.

He challenged the man on the ladder by saying, "What are you doing here?" Immediately, the man in the shrubbery pulled a gun and commanded, "Put up your hands or you are a dead man!"

Constable Barron may have hesitated or turned towards the voice but, for whatever reason, the man fired three times at the officer. Two bullets went wide of their mark, but the third struck a buckle on his suspenders, which deflected it into his side.

Badly wounded, Constable Barron turned and walked away, passing a horrified Mrs Mills and her son as he did so. He collapsed before he had gone more than a block.

At the Hamilton Hospital, doctors worked feverishly to save his life, but infection, a result of his bowel being punctured, caused a serious reversal resulting in his death 24 hours later.

Constable Barron's murder remains unsolved.

Robert Rankin

RICHARD BEASLEY
(1761-1842)
Buried in the graveyard at Christ's Church Cathedral, James Street North

The first inhabitants in the area now defined as Hamilton were probably the peace-loving Neutral Indians who called Burlington Bay *Macassa* or "shining water."

The first known white explorer in the region was René-Robert Cavelier de la Salle. With a small contingent of priests and Indians, he crossed Burlington Bay in 1669 in search of "the great western sea."

One of the original white settlers in this area was Richard Beasley. Raised in the Hudson Valley, Beasley helped establish a gristmill near what is now Ancaster in 1791.

Born of English and Dutch stock, Richard Beasley married a young woman whose family roots originated in Amsterdam. Their son, Henry, is reputed to be the first white child born in the region. Henry went on to serve in the military and in government.

Richard Beasley's careers as a merchant, land speculator and government agent were peppered with incidents involving conflict, confrontation and suggestions of unethical and possibly illegal behaviour.

Around 1793, following a dispute with the Lotteridge family, Beasley was awarded Burlington Heights, an area now occupied by Dundurn Park. His homestead was located on the present site of Dundurn Castle.

In 1798, Beasley obtained a block of land along the Grand River from the Six Nations Indians. It appears Beasley resold the land to Pennsylvania Mennonites under false pretences.

Richard Beasley did not see military action during the War of 1812. At one point, he headed a detachment of militia that searched for deserters. Later, he headed commissions to oversee the property of those who left the province and persons accused of aiding the enemy.

Beasley's own farm had strategic military value during the war and, for a period, was occupied by British troops. Beasley claimed the occupation caused destruction of his orchard and loss of crops. He was eventually offered about one-half the compensation he requested. This setback, combined with other difficulties, sent his financial affairs into a tailspin.

As a result of age and financial misfortune, Richard Beasley was compelled to sell assets. His Burlington Heights farm was sold to Sir Allan Napier MacNab who later constructed Dundurn Castle on the property.

The inscription on Richard Beasley's tombstone states he was "the first settler at the Head of the Lake."

Ronald Berenbaum

Christ's Church Cathedral, James Street North.

Sir Adam and Lady Beck.

SIR ADAM BECK
(1857-1925)
Buried in Hamilton Cemetery, 777 York Boulevard, Section N

As a boy, Adam Beck spent his play time building dikes and dams on the streams feeding his father's mill and foundry. He had worked in the family's foundry since the age of 10 and by the age of 28 he had set up his own business, producing cigar boxes for tobacco companies. He relocated his profitable business to London, Ontario, and entered local politics, becoming mayor in 1902. Beck was recruited by the Conservatives to run in the provincial election of 1902 and he won.

He married Lilian Ottaway at Christ's Church Cathedral in Hamilton in 1898, and in 1904 their only daughter Marion was born.

Beck turned his attention to making hydroelectric power a province-wide concern. The "hydro" movement had caught the imagination of the public and Beck championed the cause of cheap power for the people.

In the election of 1905, a landslide Conservative majority defeated the Liberals. One of the new government's first actions was to pass an act setting up a permanent Hydro-Electric Power Commission, the precursor to Ontario Hydro. This was the first publicly owned electric utility in the world. Adam Beck was appointed the first chairman.

To symbolize the beginning of the transmission of electricity from

Niagara to the rest of the province, Berlin (now Kitchener) was chosen for the official "switching on" ceremony. On 11 October 1910, more than 8,000 people crammed into the Queen Street arena to witness the event. Sir James Whitney, the Ontario Premier, was handed a switch on a velvet pillow. Whitney invited Beck to push the button, instantly illuminating the arena and street. A string of bulbs spelled out the words *For the People*. Beck had transformed the darkness into light.

Beck was praised as the "Human Dynamo." His single-minded determination and his image as a fighter won him admiration from the public and the government. Adam Beck was knighted for his pioneering work.

After a prolonged illness, Sir Adam Beck died on 15 August 1925. As a tribute, on the day of his funeral, electricity was suspended throughout Ontario.

Donna Reid & Robin McKee

DR GEORGE LESLIE BELL
(1890-1958)
Buried in Binbrook United Church Cemetery, Binbrook

Dr George Leslie Bell was undoubtedly one of the most respected individuals who ever lived in Binbrook. His early education was in Lincoln County; later he entered Queen's University to study medicine. Dispatches mention his service overseas in World War I. He returned home and received his medical degree in 1919.

On 4 February 1920 he married Louise Teeter of Smithville and moved into the doctor's house in Binbrook. It was the time of the influenza epidemic and he was kept very busy. When he left home his wife never knew whether she would see him that day or the next. Much of his sleep was obtained in the cutter, wrapped in his heavy coat and buffalo blankets, letting the horse find its way home. Louise was home taking telephone calls and, because very few had telephones, she had to leave messages with neighbours who had phones. A common practice was to place a white flag at the end of the lane, to signal the doctor to stop either for a patient or a message.

Bell was very active in the Masonic Order and became District Deputy Grand Master. Also, Dr Bell was on the Saltfleet-Binbrook High School Board and was instrumental in establishing a bus service for Binbrook students attending Saltfleet High School, which was a first for Ontario. He was influential in establishing the central public school system in Binbrook. Bellmoore School is in part named after him.

Dr Leslie Bell died on 10 July 1958 and his wife Louise died the next day.

On the occasion of their 25th year in Binbrook, the community honoured the couple. An illuminated address was presented to them, which reads in part,

> Through all the years, you have served the people of this community with a quiet efficiency that has won the confidence and affection of all. Professionally your work has been of the highest order as hundreds of people of this township can abundantly testify. Not only has your personal character been an inspiration but your high moral and spiritual ideals have given you a leadership in the community that is acknowledged by old and young alike. Therefore, with great unanimity and whole hearted enthusiasm, the members of the Council and the residents of the entire community desire to say "well done and splendid, Dr. Bell, for what you have done for us during these twenty-five years."

Shirley (Quance) Rumbles

SUSAN E. BENNETTO
(1850-1919)
Buried in Hamilton Cemetery, 777 York Boulevard, Section A8 & B8

Susan Bennetto became the foremost female educator of her time.

In 1867, at the age of 17 with a First-Class C teaching certificate, Susan was appointed to her first Hamilton school, with a yearly salary of $200. Her two-room framed schoolhouse was on Cannon Street East. For years, she also taught at Central School on Hunter Street West.

By 1887 Susan was engaged at the Collegiate Institute at a rate of $500 per year. On 14 June 1888 she applied for the position of head teacher or principal of the Picton Street School, then under construction at the northeast corner of Catharine and Picton Streets. She was appointed to begin the next fall at a yearly salary of $600. She was the principal at this school for more than 30 years until her death in 1919.

She was regarded as a strict disciplinarian, but was held in high regard by her students and colleagues. She was also described as a gentle and patient teacher with the gift for imparting knowledge.

Susan Bennetto taught for more than 50 years. During her tenure, she taught many prominent Hamilton citizens, including five future mayors of the city.

*Picton Street
School in 1889.*

She died in 1919. The year after her death Picton Street School was renamed in her honour. The name was later transferred to the new Bennetto Middle School that was built on Hughson Street North, which still bears her name.

Donna Reid & Robin McKee

DR THOMAS AIMERS BERTRAM
(1864-1951)
Buried in Grove Cemetery, Dundas, North Quarter

Born in 1864, Dr Tom Bertram was a quiet, beloved town doctor who, the people of Dundas would remember, had paradoxical flashes of publicity, which he shunned: his record at the Bisley Rifle Shoot of 1899; his organization of the famous Campbell rink; a memorable career in curling; and a high honour from the College of Surgeons, Dublin University, Ireland.

Think back to 1899, a time when the Dominion of Canada was defended by local militias who competed in rifle shoots — marksmanship was a highly regarded skill. Surgeon-Lieutenant Dr Tom Bertram of the 77th Battalion travelled to Britain to compete at Bisley, a famous British Empire military shooting competition, and brought home every major prize, the first man to

The Hop Bitters Trophy won by Dr TA Bertram 1899 (value 1,000 guineas)

do so from outside England.

Toronto's *Globe*, the predecessor to *The Globe and Mail*, then 14 pages long and 2 cents a copy, had the Canadian hero of Bisley sharing the front page with news of the Boer War. In Dundas, Dr Tom was met by a town ablaze with fireworks and Chinese lanterns illuminating the scarlet and gold uniforms of the militia units marching with military bands. Electricity was in its infancy, but the Collins Hotel had the Queen's initials displayed in electric light. What a celebration! A Canadian colonial had beaten 2,000 competitors from Britain and her Empire!

Dr Tom always saw the funny side of life. Once an attempt to rob a bank was frustrated by the young bankers who roomed above it. In their flight, the thieves left a can of nitroglycerine. The chief constable and Dr Tom took the liquid, poured it on the grass and set it alight. It worked! The explosion blew the windows out of the Town Hall and caused Dundas citizens much concern.

In his 60-year medical career he brought about revolutionary improvements in community health. These were the days of diphtheria, pneumonia and the dread typhoid fever and smallpox. During times of improved health conditions, he established a health service and then acted as Medical Officer of Health for 40 years.

A tragedy, never to be erased, was the loss of his only son in the Great War.

Dr Tom typified all that was splendid in the old small-town family doctor. The Dundas Museum contains medals and other mementos of his life, including the very rifle that vaulted him into such unaccustomed limelight.

Janet Brown

BINKLEY FAMILY
Buried in the Binkley Family Cemetery, Lakelet Drive, Hamilton

Binkley's Hollow, Binkley Public School, Binkley United Church, Binkley Road. Just who were the Binkleys?

The Binkley family came from Switzerland to Pennsylvania in 1735 where Marx Binkley was born in 1748. In 1780 he immigrated to Canada with his wife and five children. They stopped at the Horning House on their way and decided they liked the area so much that they would stay. They bought 800 acres of land and put up a log house at the west end of what is now Main Street West, on the north side, just before the road turns to Ancaster. Marx Binkley's tombstone in the old Binkley Cemetery in West Hamilton reads,

> *When I am dead and buried*
> *And all my bones are rotten*
> *Look on this stone and think of me*
> *Lest I should be forgotten.*

In 1802 the Binkleys built a frame house, which lasted until 1849 when it burned down. Another house was built.

The three Binkley sons inherited the farm when Marx died in 1805 and the Binkleys stayed around the area, leaving their name on churches, schools and roads. One Binkley, Jacob, became well known for organizing the Association for Detecting Horse Thieves, which was very active, catching three to ten thieves per year. Another Binkley who had been born on the farm came back to live there with his son in his old age. David Horning

Binkley, another descendant, and his wife celebrated their 60th wedding anniversary in 1910. They lived with their son across the street from the old homestead, which was sold to the Buttrum family around 1906 and eventually sold again.

The Canadian National Institute for the Blind had been looking for a place to build a new centre on and off since 1949. They eventually bought the old Binkley property in 1956 and began planning a new residence and service centre. They launched a fund drive, which proved to be highly successful, and the first sod was turned 4 November 1958. The cornerstone of Edgewood Hall was laid on 10 September 1959 and Lieutenant-Governor J. Keillor Mackay officially opened the new centre on 11 April 1960.

Margaret Houghton

JOHN JOSIAH BLACHFORD
(1820-1882)
Buried in Hamilton Cemetery, 777 York Boulevard, Section Christ's Church Cathedral — D

Miss Ona Blachford and friend in front of the Blachford & Son Funeral Parlour in 1913.

Death and the burial of the dead is a universal human preoccupation. The position of undertaker did not exist in England prior to the year 1800. Family made the required burial arrangements. The poor were buried in

shrouds. The affluent purchased coffins from local craftsmen. Bodies were buried on the family property or in a churchyard.

The profession of funeral director evolved in the latter half of the 19th century. The undertaker, usually a cabinet-maker or carpenter, provided the coffin. Over time, he often assumed responsibility for organizing the funeral procession.

By 1900, the body was often in the care of the undertaker virtually from death to burial. In North America, embalming received widespread acceptance during the U.S. Civil War. Early in the 20th century, undertakers routinely performed embalming procedures.

John Josiah Blachford was born in England 16 July 1820 and emigrated to Buffalo in 1840. In 1843, he re-located to King Street West in Hamilton, where he operated a cabinet-making and upholstery business. He also constructed and sold coffins.

By 1862, Blachford's line of products had expanded to include funereal shrouds, scarves, ribbons and crêpe. A horse-drawn hearse was available for hire. The name of the firm was changed to Blachford and Son, Undertakers and Embalmers.

The Blachfords affiliated with James Dwyer in 1881. The partnership lasted about ten years, until Dwyer established his own firm.

John Josiah Blachford died in 1882. His wife and son Charles continued to run the business. His wife died in 1903. In 1916, following the death of Charles and another brother, the firm passed out of the Blachford family and into the hands of C.H. Wray and E.G. Wray from Montreal. For many years, the firm was known as Blachford and Wray.

In 1974, Blachford and Wray aligned itself with Swackhamer and Hilts Funeral Chapel.

Ron Berenbaum

CHARLES GOODENOUGH BOOKER
(1859-1926)
Buried in Hamilton Cemetery, 777 York Boulevard, Section V

Educated locally, Charles Booker studied tailoring. When T.G. Furnival's store, where he worked, went into bankruptcy he became the new owner and made it a great success, eventually relocating it to King and John Streets.

In 1904 he was defeated as a candidate for Board of Education in Ward 1 by 38 votes. In 1906 he ran again, and this time was elected and served nine years, including one year (1915) as chairman. In 1916 he ran for mayor, but

*Edward, Prince of Wales (centre) with his good friend Charlie
Booker (left) at the opening of the Memorial School in 1919.*

no one took his candidacy seriously as he was seen as an extreme long shot.
The *Herald* newspaper gave him little hope of victory stating, "Even Mr.
Booker's closest friends refuse to take his candidature seriously." However the
two front-runners, Cooper and Morris, ran such a nasty campaign, each vili-
fying the other, that the public gravitated towards the third candidate who was
not involved with the dirty campaign. Booker was not known for his support
of the temperance movement and therefore garnered the support of those
who opposed the Ontario Temperance Act. He called it "one of the rottenest
laws ever placed on the statute books." To the great surprise of everyone,
including Booker himself, he won by a slim margin of 259 votes over Morris.

He worked during his tenure to aid the returning soldiers, being a great
supporter of the war effort. Sadly, in October of 1918 his only son was killed,
a month before amnesty was declared, and the mayor never recovered from
the blow.

During the visit from the Prince of Wales in 1919, he repeatedly (it is
reported) referred to His Royal Highness as "Princey." His ignorance of

protocol during this visit was legendary. However, the Prince must not have been terribly offended. During a subsequent visit to Canada he specifically asked after the health of his good friend Charlie Booker.

When asked about running for a third term as mayor Booker's response was typical of a man noted for his colourful language: "That third term bubbles like the vomiting of Vesuvius." In later years he ran for Board of Control and Mayor again, but never again held public office.

Margaret Houghton

MATTHEW BRITAIN
(1864-1939)
Buried in Holy Sepulchre Cemetery, 600 Spring Gardens Road, Section K

Matthew Britain, 1920.

Matthew Britain came to Hamilton from Caledonia at the age of 14 to learn the baking trade, but he soon changed to working for the Michigan Central Railway. After 12 years of that he began to look for a job that would keep him in Hamilton, and a friend suggested a job with the fire department. He was hired and assigned to Central station. A week later he was assigned to the buggy house to be the driver for Fire Chief Aitchison. He drove the Chief for the next 12 years. Or rather, he sat next to the Chief who liked to drive himself, usually at a high rate of speed.

On 5 August 1905, while speeding to a grass fire, Aitchison's buggy collided with another rig at the corner of King Street East at John Street.

Matthew Britain described the tragedy:

> I was cleaning harness when that alarm broke… and on learning it was on West Avenue South we started out, with Chief Aitchison driving. He always did drive and I just sat next to him. We went south on John Street, and the Chief decided to go to Main before going east, for West Avenue wasn't cut through between King and Main then, and just on clearing the building at King Street we saw the chemical wagon from central bearing down on us from the west. We nearly cleared it, but when the pole struck our rear wheel we were both thrown against the granite base of the monument. I was picked up for dead and taken into Wilson's shoe store, while the chief was taken away in the ambulance but I fooled them. I was out of the hospital in a month, though I've had the hiccoughs from that day, April 5, 1905, till now. The day before the accident I weighed

173 pounds, and a month later I was down to 138 and I
haven't got back much since then.

The chief died of his injuries and Britain's health was never the same.
Matthew Britain retired from the Hamilton Fire Department on 1
January 1936 after almost 33 years as an active firefighter.

Margaret Houghton

COLONEL ALEXANDER BROWN
(1776-1852)
&
MERREN (GRIERSON) BROWN
(1779-1856)

Buried in Union Cemetery, Margaret Street, Waterdown

In 1793, Alexander Brown from the Parish of Glencairn, Dumfrieshire,
Scotland, came to Montreal as an employee of the Northwest Fur Company.
Thirteen years later he moved to Upper Canada with his future brother-in-
law, James Grierson, both of them receiving large tracts of land. Brown
acquired a total of 800 acres in East Flamborough, land that stretched from
Burlington Bay northwards to above the escarpment.

When hostilities between the United States and Upper Canada began in
1812, Brown joined the local militia and rose to the rank of colonel while see-
ing service at the Battle of Lundy's Lane. During the time he was away
fighting, Indians invaded his frame house, located east of the Great Falls, and
threatened his wife, Merren, and their children, "taking every vestige of food."

On returning to Flamborough, Brown paid for the construction of a small
wooden schoolhouse and hired a teacher, Miss Mary Hopkins, to educate his
children and those in the neighbourhood. The one-room building, opened
in 1816, was one of the earliest schools in Upper Canada. In later years, following the opening of the Burlington Beach Canal, Colonel Brown and his
sons built a small wharf on the north shore of Burlington Bay to serve as a
shipping outlet for the many products that were being produced in the rapidly developing village of Waterdown.

Although Alexander Brown is recognized as the first settler in the area
that is now Waterdown, almost every resident in the village knows his name
and that of his wife because they are associated with the Waterdown Library
Ghost. In 1978 two very large tombstones commemorating the couple were

discovered on a residential construction site that had once been the home of the Waterdown Union Cemetery gravedigger. They had probably been abandoned when a new monument had been placed in Union Cemetery commemorating additional family members and correcting the spelling of Merren's name.

The monuments were rescued and a year later mounted on a downstairs wall of the old East Flamborough Township Hall, which had been converted into the village library. Since then, the mysterious ghost who haunts the elevator, which is adjacent to the tombstones, is said to be Merren's spirit, forever reminding patrons of the error in her name still visible on the original stone.

Sylvia Wray

WILLIAM BRUCE
(1832–1927)
Buried in Hamilton Cemetery, 777 York Boulevard, Section D6

William Bruce's family emigrated from Scotland to Hamilton when he was still a young boy. He attended several schools in Hamilton, including Mr McIndoe's dancing school, located in the town hall. He was originally apprenticed to Fisher & McQuesten's foundry but his health did not allow

Janet Blair Bruce in the garden of Elmwood, the Bruce home, on the mountain.

him to continue there. He tried various occupations and eventually set himself up as a patent agent.

Bruce was very artistic and some of his illuminated addresses are quite accomplished. He also wrote poetry, courting his future wife, Janet Blair, by writing numerous poems to her. One seems to be the result of an argument between the two:

> If from my lips some angry accents fell,
> Peevish complaint, or harsh reproof unkind,
> Twas but the error of a sickly mind
> And troubled thoughts, clouding the purer well,
> And waters clear, of Reason: and for me
> Let this my verse the poor atonement be.

She obviously forgave him as they married in 1853 and had three children.

Several of Bruce's brothers and sisters died of tuberculosis, and in 1869 his oldest son, Magnus, also died of the disease. Bruce then moved his family up the mountain as the air was considered to be healthier there. At Elmwood, his mountain house, he also built his own observatory, the Elmwood Observatory, which at the time was one of the finest observatories in Canada. Bruce was president of the Hamilton Astronomical Society and later their honourary president.

His younger son, William Blair Bruce, became world-famous as an artist. He had moved to Europe and was a contemporary of Chagall. Blair Bruce died in 1906 and in 1907 his father donated 32 paintings by his son to the City of Hamilton. This gift formed the nucleus of the Hamilton Art Gallery.

In 1936, nine years after her father's death, Bella Blair Walkden, his only surviving child, donated the Bruce property to the city of Hamilton. The land is now Bruce Park.

Margaret Houghton

WILLIAM BULLOCK
(1831-1912)
Buried in Christ Church Anglican Cemetery, Bullock's Corners

"One of the landmarks of this part of the country passed away on Tuesday evening at the advanced age of 81 years. William Bullock was well and favorably known to nearly everyone hereabout. For almost all his life he lived in the immediate vicinity of the place where he completed life's span. When yet a child of about two years he came to West Flamboro with his parents, from

William Bullock and his wife Sally (left) with Joseph Bullock and his wife Elizabeth (right) at Bullock's Corners.

Pennsylvania, being of good old English stock. His father established the hotel, and the place grew to be quite a hamlet and took on its name of Bullock's Corners, which it has retained to the present time. The deceased early in life engaged in the lumbering business and for some years conducted a saw mill on the Brock Road, later moving to the site now occupied by Clark's Woolen Mills. Of late years he had lived a retired life. Besides his faithful life partner [Sarah "Sally" (Kievell) Bullock], who is in her 78th year, he leaves one son, William, and one daughter, Miss Lottie. The funeral takes place on Friday afternoon to Christ Church burying ground."

Hamilton Times, 21 November 1912

JACOB BURKHOLDER
(1747–1812, 1813, OR 1817)
*Buried in the Burkholder Cemetery on Mohawk Road East
near Upper Sherman Ave.*

In 1794, Jacob Burkholder and his wife, Sophia de Roche, founded the Burkholder Settlement on the Mohawk Trail.

After the American Revolution, the Burkholder family stayed loyal to the British Crown and re-settled on the Hamilton Mountain. This established them as one of the first pioneer farm families of the area. During their first hard winter, Jacob practised tailoring and weaving, and his first customer is said to have been Peter Horning, another mountain pioneer.

One of the earliest interments in the Burkholder family's cemetery was that of Joseph Burkholder, Jacob's son, who died from a broken back after falling from a building's roof. The tombstone of Christian Burkholder (1772–1843), the eldest son of Jacob, has an interesting verse:

Burkholder United Church, Mohawk Road East, in 1944.

Remember Friend, As You Pass By,
As You are Now So Once Was I,
As I Am Now So You Will Be,
Prepare For Death And Follow Me.

As early as 1800, the people of the neighbourhood were bringing their deceased family members to the Burkholder family cemetery for burial. Because of the Burkholder's religious beliefs, no one was ever refused burial.

In 1839, land next to the cemetery was donated for the first log schoolhouse, and by 1850 the Mountain Chapel was established. Even though the buildings stood side by side with the cemetery, and were used by the same people, there was never any connection between the church and the management of the cemetery. Until 1874, the cemetery remained a family burial ground. At that time, a trustee board was established to care for the cemetery, which had begun more than 75 years earlier.

Donna Reid & Robin McKee

RICHARD BUTLER

(1834–1925)

Buried in Hamilton Cemetery, 777 York Boulevard, Section S

During the early years of the 20th century, one of Hamilton's best-known and best-loved citizens was Richard Butler.

Although not born in Hamilton, Butler came to the city seeking employ-

Hamilton's Volunteer Fire Brigade

Reminiscences of the olden days by one who carried the bucket himself.

EDITOR'S NOTE

This first article, dealing with the department of the old days of Hamilton, has been specially prepared by Mr. Richard Butler, so well known in Hamilton that it seems almost superfluous to mention details of his life. He is over 86 years of age and active in a decided manner. He is the author of the weekly Saturday Musings published in the Spectator newspaper, is a Civil War veteran, belonging to the G. A. R., and formerly Deputy U. S. Consul. This article from his pen is full of interest for all and more particularly for the older generation who will recall many of the names and incidents mentioned therein.

ment as a printer in 1849 at the age of 15. Acquiring a position with a city newspaper known as the *Journal and Express*, he later moved to the *Christian Advocate*.

In 1859, Butler and his wife Kate (née Scott) immigrated to the United States. One year later, he signed up for a three-month stint with the Union Army. In 1863 he signed up again, and served as an officer until the war's end.

Butler eventually settled in Clinton, Illinois, where he became editor and publisher of the local newspaper, the *Clinton Public*. Later, he was appointed that city's postmaster.

In 1897, Butler accepted an appointment by U.S. President William McKinley and returned to Hamilton as vice consul.

The *Hamilton Spectator* editor J. Robson Cameron knew of Butler's writing abilities. Soon after Butler arrived, he was asked to write a weekly column, which would focus on his memories of Hamilton during the 1840s and 1850s. That column, "Saturday Musings," would last more than 27 years, making Butler, who referred to himself in his writings as the Old Muser, one of Hamilton's best-known personalities.

Butler's first-hand anecdotal reminiscences of Hamilton during its early years as a city were not only popular at the time of writing, they remain wonderful sources of local historical information for researchers.

As time passed, Butler's columns evolved to cover a wider time frame. Also, the Old Muser was not hesitant to include his personal political and social views in his columns. A lifelong abstainer from the use of alcohol, Butler frequently railed against the dangers of intemperance.

Until his death at the age of 90, Butler's cheery, kindly personality was known throughout his beloved city of Hamilton.

His burial at Hamilton Cemetery was attended by a large number of its citizens. Because he was a Civil War veteran, Butler had a mournful rendition of taps played over his grave by a lone bugler.

J. Brian Henley

SARA GALBRAITH (BEEMER) CALDER
(1846-1914)
Buried in Hamilton Cemetery, 777 York Boulevard, Section D8

Mrs Sara Calder was a larger-than-life public figure. At her memorial service, Sir John Gibson, then Lieutenant-Governor of Ontario, said; "She did not know the meaning of failure and never acknowledged defeat."

Sara was the granddaughter of James and Mary Gage owners of what is now Battlefield Park in Stoney Creek. Her parents were married at the homestead.

In 1894, the Gage farmhouse and the nearby hilltop were put up for sale. The Wentworth Historical Society wanted to purchase the property. Sara wanted the site developed into a museum and a monument built to commemorate the centennial of the 1813 battle.

The male members of the historical society favoured a different location

A view of Battlefield House at the Opening of Battlefield Park by the Women's Wentworth Historical Society on 21 October 1899.

for the monument. So, in 1895, Sara founded the Ladies Committee of the Wentworth Historical Society and immediately set out to raise funds needed to buy the homestead. Sara's no-nonsense, take-charge personality came to light when her committee organized a weeklong fundraising event billed as a "military encampment." The exhibition brought in over $1400. Sara immediately broke away from the male-dominated historical society and formed the Womens' Wentworth Historical Society. The men never saw a penny from the fundraising and the new Womens' Society bought the property.

Lady Aberdeen officially opened Battlefield House and Park on 23 October 1899, and the monument was unveiled by telegraph by Queen Mary on 6 June 1913, the centennial of the Battle of Stoney Creek.

Sara Calder was also responsible for raising the funds to erect the Queen Victoria memorial statue in Gore Park, which was unveiled by Governor General Earl Grey on 25 May 1909. She was also involved with a number of organizations, including the Local Council of Women, the Victorian Order of Nurses, the Boy's Home, the Home Mission Society, the Hamilton Health Association, the Women's Art Association and the future Hamilton Art Gallery.

Sara was a devoted wife and mother to nine children.

"Larger-than-life" seems an inadequate description for this hard-driven Victorian dynamo.

Donna Reid & Robin McKee

MARTHA JULIA CARTMELL
(1845-1945)
Buried in Hamilton Cemetery, York Boulevard, Section A4

Martha Julia Cartmell was only 13 years of age when she was orphaned and came to live in Hamilton. She graduated from the Ontario Normal College in Toronto and became a teacher.

In 1874 at a Methodist missionary meeting she heard a discussion of the prospect of a foreign mission to Japan, which was beginning to open up its borders to outsiders. The Wesleyan Methodist Church sent out male missionaries who, although they were successful with the men, had no success contacting women and girls. As a result, the Women's Missionary Society was formed in 1880 and an appeal was made for a female missionary to go to Japan. Martha Cartmell had found her calling. The WMS asked her to become their first woman missionary in Japan.

She set sail for Japan on 23 November 1882, heading for an unknown

Martha Cartmell with a student in Tokyo, Japan.

country where they spoke an unknown language. She began an intensive study of the Japanese language. Soon after arrival she discovered that Japanese women did not attend school. A few were taught at home or listened to their brother's lessons but there was no opportunity for a formal education. Martha decided that she should establish a Christian school for Japanese girls. She petitioned the Imperial Court for permission and upon receiving it founded the first girls' school in Tokyo. On 6 November 1884 the Toyo Eiwa Jo Gakko opened in a small house on Torii Zaka, Asabu, with two students and three teachers. It grew tremendously with Martha Cartmell as the first principal of the school. New buildings were added and students came in increasing numbers.

When the second woman missionary arrived in Japan, Martha went out into the community and began teaching the Bible to Japanese women, eventually training many to continue the work. Ill health eventually cut short her work and she returned to Canada where she died in 1945. The school she founded is still flourishing with 1,000 students enrolled. Their school uniform bears a Canadian maple leaf on the sleeve. Each year, members of the school journey to Canada to visit Centenary Church in Hamilton, Martha Cartmell's home church, which they consider a shrine.

Margaret Houghton

Old Case Homestead near the 'Delta.' Used as a military hospital after the Battle of Stoney Creek, 6 June 1813.

DR WILLIAM CASE
(1776-1848)
*Buried in Hamilton Cemetery, 777 York Boulevard,
Section Christ's Church Cathedral — A*

Dr William Case's date of burial in the Hamilton Cemetery is 8 May 1951, more than a hundred years after his death.

William Case graduated from the Philadelphia Medical College and practised in New Hampshire before immigrating to Canada. He arrived at the Head-of-the-Lake as early as 1805, and by 1809 had settled in what is now the city of Hamilton. He cleared a farm lot on King Street near Lottridge and fitted his medical cases into his agricultural routine. It was not unusual for him to take his horse from the plough, ride for miles over roads that were mere trails to see a distant patient, and then return to his labours in the field. Patients paid their bills with produce or with services. Case noted in his account books the payments, the remedies and the patients, who included many members of early pioneer families.

Case was the first doctor in the Gore District, which included Burlington, Hamilton, Ancaster and Grimsby.

After the Battle of Stoney Creek during the War of 1812, Case's home was converted into a military hospital for two years, making it the first hospital in Hamilton.

William Case was a kindly man but held an unorthodox attitude toward religion. He considered himself an agnostic, or a person who believes that nothing is known or can be known about the existence of God or about things outside human experience. When he died in 1848 his beliefs barred him from burial in any Christian cemeteries. The family of George Hamilton allowed Case to be buried without the benefit of clergy in the Hamilton family burial grounds at the head of Ferguson Avenue. It was said that on the day of his burial a sudden thunderstorm drove the mourners for cover. The superstitious believed this to be an omen against the burial of a "free thinker" in consecrated ground.

The Hamilton family were removed from the cemetery in 1892 and relocated to the Hamilton Cemetery. In the 1950s, to eliminate the hairpin turn on the Mountain Access, Dr Case was moved as well and transferred to the Hamilton Cemetery.

Donna Reid & Robin McKee

DAVID CHAMBERS
(ca 1818-1874)
*Buried in Hamilton Cemetery, 777 York Boulevard,
Section Christ's Church Cathedral — D*

David Chambers left Biddenden, County Kent, England, on 8 March 1842 and landed in New York City on 19 April 1842. From there he went to Albany and then on to Toronto and Hamilton, arriving there on 2 May 1842. Mr Chambers was a builder and bricklayer by trade and during the first few years of his stay in Hamilton he built the first house on Bay Street North. This house, on the west side of Bay Street, is still standing between Barton and Stuart Streets. Chambers put the ends of bottles around all the windows and doors. It was quite a sight and led to the house being called Bottle House. Later the bottles were removed and the house, which was frame, was fixed over. This was not his greatest claim to fame in Hamilton, however. Winter was a slow season for builders so David Chambers, having done some bird mounting in England, occupied himself as a taxidermist during his off-season.

He mounted two toads on their hind legs, placing little swords, and posed them as if they were fighting. He made one large bird out of part of a pheasant, part of a chicken and part of something else that was not readily identifiable. He stuffed a horse for a saddler's shop and once stuffed a 35-pound turkey.

One time he stuffed a wildcat, put it on wheels and ran along the street pulling the cat behind him. The newspaper reported the next day, "Mr.

David Chambers with some of his handiwork.

David Chambers ran down King Street pursued by a wild cat." He was also very fond of children and often took hordes of small boys out kite flying.

David Chambers died very suddenly of a fit of apoplexy on 11 May 1874. The *Hamilton Spectator* reported at his death he was possessed of considerable property: "Only a few weeks ago, he purchased a vacant lot upon which he had commenced erecting a valuable building for a homestead, but an all-wise Providence declared otherwise." He was buried with the customary honours of his fraternity, the Odd Fellows.

Margaret Houghton

THOMAS CHOATE
(1773-1859)
Buried in St Paul's Glanford Anglican Church cemetery, Glanford

Thomas Choate was born 23 January 1773, in what is now Essex, Massachusetts. He was the fifth generation of Choates to live there since the original Choate, John, emigrated from Sudbury, England, to America in 1643. When Thomas was young, his parents moved to New Hampshire. Thomas was not a United Empire Loyalist, but in 1798 he took advantage of Governor Simcoe's offer of free land in Upper Canada. He came with three brothers and two cousins. He was the second settler to take up land in the township of Glanford. He married Anna McCarter, granddaughter of Robert Land, in 1808. They were to have fifteen children.

During the War of 1812, he fought against his former countrymen and served under General Brock at the battle of Queenston Heights.

Thomas became a very successful farmer. He was very interested in his cattle and horses and improving his stock. Thomas was among the first to engage in butter- and cheese-making in this part of Upper Canada. Over the years he acquired extensive land holdings and by 1841 owned 1,284 acres. He built his final home probably in the years 1814–16. It still stands on the east side of Highway #6, south of White Church Road. Now a huge radio tower stands in front of it.

Thomas's son, also named Thomas, became the first clerk of Glanford Township. He held that position for 40 years. He guided the elected councillors well. He became known as the Father of Glanford Township.

Thomas the elder had another son, Joseph Birney Choate, who donated the land for St Paul's Glanford Anglican Church.

Thomas the elder died 7 March 1859 at the age of 86 years. He lies buried in St Paul's Glanford cemetery. His tombstone has been vandalized twice in the last 20 years and now presents a sorry-looking sight. This pioneer deserves more respect than this.

Bill Brigham

CHOLERA VICTIMS

Memorial in Hamilton Cemetery, 777 York Boulevard

The flow of emigrants to Hamilton in the 1830s proved disastrous, as they brought with them one of the greatest scourges of the time: cholera. The emigrant faced not only the threat of the disease but also the antagonism of the inhabitants. John Glasgow arrived from Scotland in the latter part of 1832 and describes his reception after spending his first night under the open air on the wharf:

> As we wended our way up over the mud road as far as what is now called Macauley Street we found ourselves to be in the woods, and on a dilapidated corduroy road, with a pretty steep bank at the southern terminus of the wooden macadam... we... reached the locality of what is now Stuart Street... On inquiry it was found impossible to procure a dwelling to move into, on account of our having come through the cholera district. The immigrant shed, in the northeast part of the town, seemed too filthy to enter. By the time we reached the wharf on our return Bella Little had been seized by the fell monster and died... and the corpse was laid in mother earth at the Methodist Church... on the corner of King and Wellington streets, the only public burying ground in the town at that time. On our return to our headquarters at the wharf, Mr. Gunn and Mr. Vallance, his clerk, took pity on us, and kindly had us placed in the storehouse, under cover. Mr. George Little, who had just married his young wife before leaving Scotland, and who seemed to be in perfect health, when he returned from the mournful and sad rite performed over the remains of his deceased sister, he, too, was taken sick at 10 o'clock that night, and died at 2 o'clock next morning. The townspeople, though very kind, were alarmed, and were fully aware of the danger of coming in contact with us. Mr. George Hamilton... most kindly and thoughtfully suggested that we should build a shanty at the edge of the woods about 150 yards south of the Court House... We took advantage of the offer, and the remaining members of the families moved into their new abode... We lived there until the cold weather set in.

Approximately 142 victims died during this onslaught. In an attempt to stop the spread, the slaughterhouses were closed and washed down with lime, a separate cholera hospital was built and new emigrants were segregated. One person out of every 20 died.

Margaret Houghton

REVEREND THOMAS CHRISTIE
(1783-1870)
Buried in West Flamborough Presbyterian Church Cemetery, Christie's Corners, West Flamborough Township

In 1832, Reverend Thomas Christie, a Presbyterian missionary from Holm in the Orkney Islands, Scotland, volunteered to come to Upper Canada to lead church work in the colony. He arrived at Quebec in late summer during the height of the cholera epidemic, contracted the often-fatal disease and survived.

A year later he responded to a call from a congregation of pioneer settlers in the Flamborough area:

> We the undersigned members of the Presbyterian Church of West Flamboro and Beverly and the neighbouring townships... being destitute of the privileges of the Gospel and earnestly desirous of possessing them, and being persuaded by good report and our own experience of the fitness for the work of the ministry of you, Rev. Thomas Christie, missionary... invite, entreat and call you to become our pastor.

With Christie's acceptance of the invitation, a small wooden church was erected on the Stone Road, close to the boundary between Beverly and West Flamborough Townships. Besides serving the Flamborough church, Rev. Christie preached throughout the southern part of Upper Canada, travelling as far east as Kingston and as far north as Fergus. Many of these settlements were a day's travel apart, but his commitment to establish congregations helped to overcome the loneliness and hardships he faced. On one occasion, he and the Rev. William Proudfoot of London walked to Goderich and back, gathering groups of converts along the way and meeting with them for encouragement on their return.

During the years Christie undertook missionary work, the church in West

Flamborough continued under his care. At a meeting in December 1857, the congregation recognized his work by raising his stipend from £125 to £150 per annum.

The increasing size of the congregation created the need for a new church by 1865, and when it opened on 17 February 1867, Rev. Christie conducted the first morning service. The following Monday evening, during a tea meeting held to raise money to eliminate the remaining debt on the new building, William Henderson read an address to the minister and presented him with a purse containing $200 as a token of their esteem.

Rev. Thomas Christie continued his duties as pastor of the congregation until a few days before his death on 8 September 1870 at 87 years of age. He was buried in the church cemetery, close to the spot where the altar in the original church had stood.

Sylvia Wray

JAMES COLEMAN
(1810-1881)
Buried in Grove Cemetery, Dundas, South Quarter

The rowboat started to take in water as the steamer Argyle passed, and it rocked it in its wake. The three young ladies panicked, stood up and tipped over the boat, spilling themselves and the two young men with them into the waters of the Desjardins Canal. Four of them drowned, including siblings Edwin and Caroline Coleman, the son and daughter of Dundas merchant James Coleman. For Mr Coleman, that 12th day of June 1865 was the worst of a series of tragedies that tested a truly blessed and cursed life.

James Coleman's Dundas residence, 1851.

Born in Ireland, he arrived in Dundas in 1832 seeking his fortune. He started with a small general store on Main Street and eventually became the most successful merchant in Dundas, importing and exporting large varieties and quantities of goods. He owned ships, factories and mills, and was the town's mayor from 1850 to 1852.

But, along with his fortunes, he had more than his share of misfortunes. When wheat prices collapsed following the end of the Crimean War, Mr Coleman experienced a substantial financial setback. But that was nothing compared to the loss of two of his children, including son Edwin, his heir apparent, on that fateful day on the canal. The conclusion of the American Civil War later the same year saw another economic depression, which resulted in another financial setback. The fourth major disaster in his life was the burning down of his beautiful home, the largest in Dundas, in 1869. He rebuilt it at once, but as the depression continued he was driven into bankruptcy and lost his home in 1872. He moved to Hamilton and organized the Hamilton Iron Forging Works, which he managed until his death on 6 March 1881.

His funeral was a lavish affair befitting a man who lived life large; mourners were transported in sleighs from Hamilton to Grove Cemetery where he was buried alongside his wife and the six children who predeceased him.

James Coleman was a big man with a big heart, and he did everything in a big way. His indefatigable spirit allowed him to overcome tragedies that would have set back a lesser individual. It also allowed him to achieve phenomenal successes that enriched his life as well as the lives those around him, and left a memorable imprint on Dundas history.

Stan Nowak

WILLIAM COOK
(ca 1822-1877)
Buried in St Alban's the Martyr Anglican Church Cemetery, Rockton

In the St Alban's churchyard there is a tombstone standing alone, in an unconsecrated area. The tombstone is inscribed *"William Cook, died February 5, 1877, a native of Cornwall, England."*

William Cook, a farmer, lived on the 5th concession of the Township of Beverly, together with his wife, Elizabeth, and three unmarried daughters. His son, John, lived across the road on a second property. William leased his farm property from the estate of the late Thomas Ireland, but he was very dissatisfied with this lease, his crops not having proved as remunerative as he could have wished. William had a very violent temper and he was constantly quarrelling with the members of his family. At various times he threatened to do violence to his family, particularly his eldest daughter whom he believed was thinking of leaving the parental home. Cook went into his house and asked for some lead, saying that he wished to load the gun to shoot something in the yard. Failing to obtain what he wanted, he went out but shortly returned and leveled the gun at his eldest daughter, discharging the contents into her side. Son John, hearing the shotgun blast, rushed over to the family home and tried to administer aid to his sister who was lying on the floor, bleeding profusely. John summoned a neighbour and both set off to find the father William. The found him lying behind the barn with the entire top and back of his head blown off. Cook had reloaded the gun, tied a rope to the trigger and put his foot into a loop of the rope, by which means he had discharged the contents into his head.

Cook died immediately but his daughter lingered at death's door for three days, finally dying of her wounds on 7 February 1877, age 23. Maria was properly buried in the consecrated area of the cemetery but William was denied the benefit of a Christian burial, even though he was a churchwarden of St Alban's Church, Rockton.

This should prove a lesson to all who are possessed of unruly tempers to endeavour to curb their passions, as there can be no doubt that Cook was perfectly sane, and that the murder of his own daughter and the act of suicide were committed while in a passion.

Viola M. Collins

WILLIAM WINER COOKE
(1846-1876)
Buried in Hamilton Cemetery, 777 York Boulevard,
Section Christ's Church Cathedral — B

Although born in Mount Pleasant, near Brantford, William Winer Cooke had strong Hamilton connections, particularly as his mother, Angeline Augusta Winer Cooke, came from one of the Ambitious City's leading families. William Cooke would also attend Central Public School in Hamilton before he began his military career. As did over 50,000 other Canadians, William Winer Cooke crossed the border into the United States to participate in the Civil War.

Although he claimed to be 22 years of age, Cooke was actually just 18 when he arrived in Rochester to enlist with the 24th New York Cavalry. Cooke saw some action in the war and did receive some wounds before he mustered out of the Union Army on 25 June 1865.

While it is not certain whether Cooke had met George Armstrong Custer during the war, it is certainly possible that he did.

In any case, Cooke did indeed join the 7th U.S. Cavalry in 1866 and served with Custer during the military campaigns against native peoples in Montana and other areas of the American plains.

Cooke and Custer had become close friends. Once, when both were on leave, Custer accompanied Cooke to Hamilton when the latter came home to visit friends and family. The arrival of the famous Civil War general and his Canadian friend caused a sensation in Hamilton. A huge crowd gathered at the Great Western Railway station to greet them.

William Winer Cooke was only 36 years old when he, along with over 200 other soldiers, was killed at the Little Big Horn at the famous massacre, which took place on 25 June 1876.

When the news of Cooke's death reached Hamilton, there was a great outpouring of sorrow. A special service was held at Christ's Church during which Cooke was eulogized as a hero.

Just over three weeks later, Cooke's remains arrived for burial in the Winer family plot of Hamilton cemetery. With a large assemblage in attendance, William Winer Cooke was buried with full military honours.

J. Brian Henley

DAVID COULTER
(1854-1936)

Buried in Hamilton Cemetery, 777 York Boulevard, Section A6, B6

David Coulter (left) and his colleague, patrolman Harris, driving Canada's first "paddy wagon" in 1884.

Rising from a beat constable to police chief, David Coulter served his adopted city of Hamilton on its police force for 58 years.

Born in Ulster, Ireland, Coulter immigrated to Hamilton with his family about 1860.

He joined the police department in March 1878, when Hamilton's population was about 40,000 but policed by only 40 men.

Coulter was chosen as Hamilton's first patrol wagon driver in 1884. Previously, inebriates too drunk to walk were often hauled to jail in a wheelbarrow. Hamilton's police force was the first in Canada to purchase a patrol wagon to do such work with more efficiency.

A tall, very strong, intelligent individual, Coulter earned the respect of his peers on the police force, as well as that of any two-fisted street fighter who might have been tempted to arouse his ire.

In 1911, he was appointed inspector with the newly formed East End division. Operating the station on Sherman Avenue North, Coulter was credited with bringing a measure of law and order to a previously troublesome district where large numbers of single men, most recent immigrants to the city, lived and worked in the heavy industrial plants.

Every Christmas, Coulter and his men at the Sherman Avenue Station also organized a Christmas distribution of gifts and food to needy families in the area.

In an article about the East End division, appearing in the *Hamilton Herald* on 31 August 1912, Coulter was described as "one of the most potent forces in the East End in educating foreigners in Canadian citizenship."

David Coulter became Hamilton's Deputy Police Chief in 1915, then moved into the Police Chief's position on 23 April 1924.

Barely two months into his retirement, David Coulter died at his home after a brief struggle with cancer. He was 81 years old.

After the funeral service at Ryerson United Church, an impressive procession was formed. Behind the hearse was an escort of uniformed Hamilton policemen on motorcycles, about 90 Hamilton policemen on foot and representatives from municipal, provincial and railway police forces from across the nation. A contingent of Royal Canadian Mounted Policemen in their scarlet tunics added a dash of colour to the procession.

Large numbers of citizens lined the streets to pay their respects to one of Hamilton's most famous and longest serving police officers.

J. Brian Henley

HERBERT DAVIS
(1871-1952)
Buried in Grove Cemetery, Dundas, Oak Hill Section

In January 1919, following a bitter municipal election campaign, Mayor Herbert Davis and the entire Dundas Town Council were voted out of office. With nearly 1,000 votes being cast, Samuel Lennard defeated the incumbent Herb Davis by 330 votes.

The Dundas Town Hall.

It was the first time a mayor had been deposed after only one year in office. Never before had a new council been elected with members of the old council still standing. The work of the old council played no part in the election; the entire issue revolved around the Park question. It was the one that decided the election.

Town council intended to sever the western side of the Dundas Driving Park to allow J.W. Lawrason to build a row of homes on the site. With the town's population increasing, the deal would allow building lots to become available. Mayor Davis stated, "from council's perspective it was a good deal" and one he strongly supported.

Leading the charge against the Parkside Survey was the town's federal Member of Parliament, Gordon Wilson. In an open letter to the *Dundas Star* he voiced his opposition and urged the Parkside deal be annulled. Returning from Ottawa, he stated that Lawrason was "putting one over on the town." Wilson threatened an injunction and vowed to kick council out of office.

On 3 January 1919 a meeting was held in the Music Hall, with Gordon Wilson as speaker. As the recognized leader of the opposition forces he campaigned vigorously. A slate of candidates opposed to the Parkside Survey was endorsed unanimously.

The next day a letter signed by Mayor Davis and members of council was delivered to every home in Dundas. The letter reviewed the year's work of council and addressed concerns surrounding the Parkside Survey. All to no avail. With Gordon Wilson leading the charge, Mayor Davis and all members of town council were swept from office. Wilson had made good his boast.

In a hall leading to the council chambers of the Dundas Town Hall are photographs of those citizens who have held the town's highest elected office. Davis, still angry after his 1919 election defeat, refused to allow his photograph to hang in this gallery of distinction. Only after his death in 1952 did his daughter place his photograph in its rightful place.

Clare Crozier

JOHN BURWELL DAVIS
(1861–1952)
Buried in the Stoney Creek Cemetery

John Burwell Davis was descended from the Loyalist family that settled Mount Albion in 1790. At the turn of the 20th century, John Burwell Davis was a pillar of the community of Stoney Creek. Known as J.B. to his friends, he was involved in many aspects of life in the small village, from society to politics to religion.

Albion Mill Falls in Mount Albion.

As a young man, Davis was a travelling salesman, primarily arranging agricultural equipment deals with farmers in Canada and the U.S. in the 1880s. Having close experience with farmers and an inquisitive mind, he patented several farm equipment inventions of his own, including a belt-drive fanning mill in 1879, a diamond mesh screen and the J.B.D. Cockle Hurdle.

Returning to Saltfleet Township for good in the 1890s, he settled in the village and worked in a variety of positions, including stationmaster for the new Toronto, Hamilton & Buffalo Railway station in Stoney Creek in 1897. Davis also managed several small industries, including a planing mill. He married in 1890, and he and his wife Alice had two children. He also was part of the building team for the Anglican Redeemer Church in 1878. He joined the local Masonic Lodge and became master of the lodge in 1908.

A prominent Tory, Davis was closely linked to E.D. Smith and succeeded the senator as president of the Stoney Creek Literary Society. In 1915, J.B. was appointed Justice of the Peace for Wentworth. This was his second application, the first having been rejected despite backing from notables like Smith.

Davis was the first magistrate to try speeding cases on the new Toronto–Hamilton highway (now the QEW). He served as Justice of the Peace until 1935.

Despite his workload, Davis was continuously involved in his community, and aided neighbours. He fell off the roof of the barn of A.E. Jones in 1931, and never fully recovered his health.

Not given to modesty, he fought even posthumously for his place in annals of Stoney Creek history. The final line in his biography is a pre-emptive rebuttal to the potential critics of his life: "I hereby challenge you to do the same and there will be lines to skip in your life too."

Michael Gemmell

ALMA (LEITH) DICK LAUDER
(1854-1942)
Buried in St John's Anglican Church Cemetery, Ancaster

Alma Dick Lauder was one of the most colourful people ever to have lived in Ancaster. She was a writer, and contributed most of the writing in *Wentworth Landmarks* (1897). Although she was born in Hamilton, the youngest child of George Gordon Browne Leith and his wife Eleanor Ferrier, her parents soon moved to their new country home, The

Hermitage, west of Ancaster near the Sulphur Spring. This beautiful property influenced her for the rest of her life. She married Stair Dick Lauder in 1878, against the wishes of her parents, and the marriage did not last.

Her writings, almost entirely unpublished, began when she was 12 years old, and continued with diaries and hundreds of letters. In 1896, she wrote a series of historical articles for the *Hamilton Spectator*, under the title "Delving Among Ruins." Eight of these articles, with a number by other local writers, were published in 1897 in book form as *Wentworth Landmarks*. She describes the Ancaster churches and their graveyards, and mills and houses that were falling into ruin. Farther afield, in Barton, she writes of the old Terryberry Inn and a "forgotten house of peace," the Hess burying ground. She stated in her diary that she loved talking to old people about old times, and her interest in the area's past is clear.

When she moved to The Hermitage, she lived alone, delighting in this beautiful property. Many local people remember her peculiar way of life in her later years. There are stories of tea parties in the faded elegance of the drawing room, where guests, cats and chickens partook of their meals together. On 10 October 1934, at a luncheon party, fire completely consumed the mansion, but neighbours managed to save a good deal of the furnishings, paintings and books on the ground floor. Mrs Dick Lauder, who had been nothing all her life if not resourceful, had a small house constructed inside the stone walls, and here she lived until her death in 1942. Her wish

The living room of The Hermitage after the fire of 1934.

was to be buried on the estate, under the oaks on the turn in the avenue, but she was interred instead in St John's Churchyard.

Paul Grimwood

JOHN DICKENSON
(1847–1932)
Buried in North Glanford Cemetery, Glanbrook

John Dickenson arrived in Glanford, Upper Canada, in 1858 with his parents, two brothers and a sister. John's father, Edward, began a construction business and was joined by his two sons, John and Edward, while they

DeCew Falls, near St. Catharines, was Hamilton's first source of hydroelectric power.

were still in their early teens. John was best known as a politician and entre-preneur: township councillor, reeve, county warden and MLA for Wentworth South for 12 years from 1892 to 1904; one of the Five Johns who brought electricity to Hamilton in 1896 from Decew Falls; a founder of the Bank of Hamilton.

Only locally was he known as one of the founding fathers of the Glanford Curling Club, established in 1894. John bought a small property on the east side of the present Homestead Drive in Mount Hope, land so low as to be virtually useless for agriculture. Curling was another matter.

John built the original two-sheet rink, which opened for curling in the fall of 1895. To promote the new village activity, John donated a 30-inch-high sil-ver-plated trophy for competition in South Wentworth, appropriately won by Glanford in 1896, the first year of play for this magnificent trophy. Although John owned the land and donated a trophy to the game, his brother, Ed, was the club president from 1897 to 1915. John's son, J. Herbert, was then elected president and served until his death in 1918. John then decided that the curl-ing club should pay $75 per year for rent for the club. In an apparent countermove, the membership voted in John as club president for the rest of the 1918–19 season. It did no good. The rent of $75 stood.

At the annual meeting in the fall of 1919, John Dickenson was rejected as president, along with vice-president John Macdonald. A battle over the rent appeared to be settling in. In a mellower mood, in 1920, the membership made John Dickenson an honorary president, but the rent of $75 still stayed in place.

John may have persuaded the voters in political affairs that he was the right person, but it appears he ran into a different "electorate" in the curling world.

Art French

JAMES JOSEPH EVEL
(1849–1932)
Buried in Hamilton Cemetery, 777 York Boulevard, Section Q

James Evel was born in Plymouth, England, and apprenticed there to a cabinet-maker. Cabinet-makers quite often got into the trade of casket-making, as the demand was constant and the work guaranteed. After his seven-year apprenticeship was up, he immigrated to Canada. Upon his arrival in Hamilton he worked briefly for the railway before returning to his calling as a cabinet- and casket-maker.

In 1879 the Provincial Exhibition was held in Hamilton's Crystal Palace on the grounds of Victoria Park. All manner of manufactured goods from

Canada and the United States were featured, including samples of cloth-covered caskets from a manufacturer in Buffalo. At this time free trade allowed the easy passage of American goods over the border and few manufacturers could compete with the cheap American products. Evel was heard to say, "I believe I could make as fine caskets if I could only compete with the Buffalo people." He was overheard by possibly the only person who could do something about that, the visiting prime minister, Sir John A. Macdonald, who reportedly turned to Evel and said, "You think you could do as well with the work if you only were protected from competition. I will see what can be done to help you." Whether this was the impetus for the change or not, Macdonald's government soon changed the national policy to protect local manufacturers, and Canadian casket-making became a profitable business.

The Semmens and Evel Casket Company, established in 1879 by the Semmens Brothers and incorporated in 1906, became the largest plant of its kind in the Dominion. They had a staff of more than 100 employees and seven travelling salesmen. The plant, located on Florence Street across from Victoria Park, had a total floor space of 75,000 square feet. They carried an enormous stock of goods, often with more than 5,000 caskets and coffins in stock.

After a falling out with his partners in Semmens and Evel, in 1908 James Evel set up his own business, the Evel Casket Company on York Street. This plant was three storeys high, with each floor containing 20,000 square feet. They made a specialty of solid oak caskets and men's and women's shrouds, and employed 30 workmen and three travelling salesmen.

Margaret Houghton

FLORENCE "FLOSS" ELLIOT WARBURTON FARMER
(1879-1974)
Buried in St John's Anglican Church Cemetery, Ancaster

Florence Farmer was the fifth daughter of William Farmer and Elizabeth Wyly of Elizabeth, New Jersey. Her father, William, was a son of the first William Farmer to come to Canada in 1834. The family arrived in Ancaster in the 1860s. William Jr was an architect and engineer, and practised in New York City. However he moved his family back to Ancaster in 1881, where they lived at Brockton and could be educated in Canada. Florence graduated from Jarvis Street Collegiate, Toronto, in 1897, later attending the Toronto Conservatory of Music. In 1908 she graduated from the Brooklyn Hospital as a nurse, and took up private duty nursing in New York while she earned a postgraduate degree in social service.

During World War I, she served with the American Red Cross Society, and left for Europe on the Red Cross mercy ship in September 1914. She was first posted to the military hospital in Kiev in 1914. Czar Nicholas officiated at its opening, and she shook the Emperor's hand. Her Majesty Empress Feodorovna, on behalf of the Imperial Government of Czar Nicholas, later presented her with the St George silver medal with the St Andrew's Ribbon. Later posts included hospitals in Khoi, Persia (1915-16), in Shanghai, China and in the Czecho-American Hospital, Tumern, Siberia.

In the spring of 1918, because of the scarcity of food in Petrograd, wealthy parents sent 780 children to a summer camp in the Ural Mountains. The fighting forced the children eastward on to the Siberian plains, passing through Ekaterinburg where the Imperial family was being held captive. Gradually, money ran out, but the American Red Cross succeeded in moving them to an island near Vladivostock. They were sent by Japanese freighter to San Francisco, through the Panama Canal to New York City, on to France and finally to Finland. There, they were housed in a large Sanatorium at Halila, 30 miles from the Russian border. The last of the children were reunited with their families on 26 January 1921. Florence Farmer had been with them the whole time.

Her later years were spent in New York City and Ancaster, where she owned both Deerspring on the Sulphur Springs Road and the stone house on Wilson Street that was later lived in by artist Frank Panabaker. At age 85, she was still working as a private duty nurse, but retired to Hamilton in 1972.

Paul Grimwood

BRIGADIER-GENERAL GEORGE RICHARD DEVEY FARMER, C.B.E., K. ST. J., M.D.
(1896-1971)
Buried in St John's Anglican Church Cemetery, Ancaster

Richard Devey Farmer was born in Ancaster in 1896, son of Dr George Devey Farmer and Eleanor Shelton Devey Farmer, who were first cousins.

Richard was educated at Central Collegiate in Hamilton and, from 1911, spent two years at Upper Canada College, Toronto. Medical school followed at the University of Toronto, where students were encouraged to stay during World War I years until graduation, as the country would have need of more doctors. Upon his graduation in 1918, he went to England, where he met his father for the first time since the latter had gone overseas in 1915. His father suggested that he study neurology at the University of Paris "to grow up." After graduation, he returned to Canada, married Margaret Champ, and set up medical practice in Hamilton at the corner of Herkimer and Caroline Streets.

Brigadier-General Farmer (top row, second from right) with (seated) General Crerar (second from left), Winston Churchill (third from left), and General Montgomery (far right).

In 1939, at the outbreak of World War II, he assumed command of the same 5th Field Ambulance as had been commanded by his father, and went overseas in December of that year. In 1941 he assumed command of the 15th Canadian General Hospital (the Toronto General Hospital Overseas). He served in both Africa and Italy in 1943 and, returning to England in 1944, became a Brigadier and Director of Medical Services for the 2nd Canadian Corps under Lieutenant General Guy Simonds. This corps was part of the Normandy invasion, and Dr Farmer served in France, Holland and Germany, wintering in Nijmegen in 1945.

A remarkable photograph exists of Dr Farmer with Viscount Alanbroke, Sir Winston Churchill, Viscount Montgomery of Alamein, General Henry Crerar, Lt Gen Guy Simonds and the other service chiefs, posed together before the Normandy invasion.

On his return to Canada, Dr Farmer served in Ottawa with the Department of Veterans' Affairs, Hospital Section. He retired to Ancaster in May 1971, but died in July of that year of a heart attack.

Paul Grimwood

COLIN CAMPBELL FERRIE
(1808-1856)
Buried in the Hamilton Cemetery, 777 York Boulevard, Section F4

The first mayor of Hamilton came from fine Scottish lineage, or so it was thought. He and his father were hard-working Scots, but their ancestors were Spanish. In 1588, Admiral Ferrier commanded a ship in the Spanish Armada. After defeat by the British, facing death if he returned home, the enterprising Ferrier headed for Scotland. He traded in his ship and his doubloons for a new identity.

From that ignominious beginning a dynasty of merchants was created. At the age of 16, Colin immigrated to Montreal to handle the family's wholesale operation. In 1826, spurred on by rapid population growth in Hamilton, he and his two brothers relocated to the Head-of-the-Lake community. Here they established C. and J. Ferrie and Company. They sold their groceries, dry goods, stationery and hardware from a store on King Street. Goods were imported through their main supplier, and father, Adam Ferrie in Montreal. The business grew rapidly. Within seven years there were stores in Brantford, Galt, Nelson, Dundas and Waterloo.

Colin Ferrie was active in many commercial enterprises. He was a founding member of both the Gore Bank and the Hamilton Board of Trade. He held the presidency of the bank from 1839 until his death.

*The Gore Bank,
King Street
East.*

His involvement with the community led to an active career in politics. He chaired the Board of Health during the cholera epidemics of 1832 and later joined Hamilton's first police board. In 1836 he was elected to the House of Assembly. Ferrie was chosen Hamilton's first mayor in 1847, when he was only 39 years old.

Donna Reid & Robin McKee

CLEMENTINA (TRENHOLME) FESSENDEN
(1844-1918)
Buried in St John's Anglican Church Cemetery, Ancaster

Clementina Fessenden came to Ancaster in 1893 with her husband Elisha, when he accepted the post of rector at St John's Anglican Church in Ancaster. They were both intensely interested in history and the concept of the imperial ties that Canada had with the rest of the Commonwealth. They worked together in the Wentworth Historical Society and were jointly honoured by the society in 1896 for their contributions. That same year Clementina was widowed. Struck by the enthusiasm of her granddaughter, she got the idea of linking imperialism, patriotism and education through a participatory Empire Day, to be celebrated in all Canadian schools. She began a tireless campaign towards that end, writing to any and all that she thought could help her in her quest.

Empire Day was first observed in 1898 at Dundas, on the last school day before Queen Victoria's birthday, on 24 May. It spread more each year and was instituted in England in 1904. By 1913 a typical programme took up the whole school day, with music, recitations, songs and inspirational speeches. For Empire Day 1917, 64 Dominion flags were massed in St Paul's Cathedral, London, England.

In 1901 Clementina Fessenden became the first curator of Dundurn Castle, and the first chapter of the Imperial Order Daughters of the Empire in Hamilton was named the Fessenden Chapter. All of her causes were not winning ones, however, as during World War I she spoke out vehemently against women's suffrage. She felt that giving women the vote would weaken the bonds of family life and thus shake the cornerstone of Empire. If women were granted the vote, she said, it would be the "beginning of a sex war including sex hatred that shall undermine the very foundations of the home." She died in 1918 and was one of the first people in Hamilton to be taken to their final resting place in a motorized hearse. Women did get the vote, but she did not live to see it.

Margaret Houghton

KATE FIELD
(1869-1873)
&
WILLIAM FIELD
(1872-1873)
Buried in Hamilton Cemetery, 777 York Boulevard,
Section Christ's Church Cathedral — C

On the morning of 12 June 1873 Thomas Field committed an act that horrified the people of Hamilton. His family and acquaintances knew him as a violent and abusive man who drank to excess. He was married to his second wife, Jane, and lived with her and her daughter, Kate, four years of age, from a previous marriage, as well as their son, William, 14 months of age.

The previous night Field had drunk himself into a stupor. The next morning his wife awoke to find him attacking her with a hatchet. After a struggle, in which her head was badly cut, she managed to grab the hatchet and run out of the house for help. Field was next seen standing casually in the doorway of the house smoking his pipe. A policeman, hearing that Field had assaulted his wife, questioned him. Field pulled a knife out of his pocket and the policeman noticed that it had blood on it. He asked Field where his children were, to which Field replied, "I suppose that they are dead by this time." The constable took Field to jail and then returned to search the house. He found the two children lying in a pool of blood with their throats cut, murdered by their father. Thomas Field was committed to jail to await trial for murder. The two young victims were buried together in Hamilton Cemetery.

On 7 September 1873 Field asked for a prayer-book. The turnkey of the jail returned later with the prayer-book to find Thomas Field hanging by the neck by a piece of bed sheet from the grating of his cell. He left a note which read in part,

> My dear wife, I forgive you all that you have said and done to me, and I hope that God will forgive you and that you will give yourself to God and live a religious woman the rest of your days and never let that angry temper of yours get the best of your better judgment. Good-bye and God bless you and keep you from harm forever. Your affection-ate husband, T. Field

A coroner's jury later returned a verdict that Field came to death by hanging, perpetrated by his own hands.

About 1944, vandals stole the tombstone of the Field children from Hamilton Cemetery.

Margaret Houghton

JOHN CHARLES FIELDS
(1863-1932)
Buried in Hamilton Cemetery, 777 York Boulevard, Section A7

John Fields was one of the world's foremost mathematicians of his time and originated an award in mathematics that is considered the equivalent of a Nobel Prize. John was born and raised in Hamilton. He studied at the University of Toronto, graduated in 1884 and then earned his Ph D at Johns Hopkins University. He returned to Toronto in 1902 as a math professor, where he taught until his death.

He traveled the world and was well acquainted with several monarchs, Pope Pius XII and Benito Mussolini.

Fields was a firm believer in academic research and lobbied the governments to launch the National Research Council and the Ontario Research Foundation.

His greatest legacy is the medal that bears his name. In 1932, he bequeathed $47,000 for an award to be granted every four years. It was to be awarded to a mathematician under the age of 40, to encourage development of promising researchers. The medal is considered the equal to the Nobel Prize and is truly Canadian. The movie, *Good Will Hunting*, is loosely based on a savant janitor being encouraged to pursue the Fields Medal.

Donna Reid & Robin McKee

GEORGE THOMAS FRENCH
(1886-1947)
Buried in St Paul's Glanford Anglican Church, Mount Hope

George Thomas French was born 29 June 1886, most likely in Barton Township. His father, Francis French, had lived in Glanford Township all his life until about 1884 or 1885, when he moved to Long's Corners, Barton, as a blacksmith. George was the middle of five children. Sadly, his two older sisters died within two weeks of each other, six months before George was born.

His first career was with the CNR, qualifying as a train engineer at age 21. He was the youngest to qualify up to that time. In 1914, he purchased the J.R. McKichan Company, a wholesale paper business that had started in 1867, the year of Confederation. In 1873, the company was making paper bags at 32 James Street South, Hamilton. The business moved its location over the years and is presently located on Nebo Road, on Hamilton Mountain.

G.T. was active in many fields. He was a 32nd-degree Scottish Rite Mason and a member of Erie Lodge A.F. and A.M. in Port Dover. He was a member of the Victoria Curling Club in Hamilton as well as a member of the Hamilton Chamber of Commerce. He lived in Hamilton all his life and belonged to St Peter's Anglican Church. Despite his larger city connections, George Thomas French was buried in St Paul's Glanford Church Cemetery, where his parents and grandparents were interred decades earlier.

After his death in 1947, his family operated the company until 1971. The company has passed into private ownership but the name has been kept with the added phrase "Established 1867."

Art French

The interior of Battlefield House in 1913.

JAMES GAGE
(1774-1854)
Buried in Hamilton Cemetery, 777 York Boulevard, Section C3

James Gage was born in New York to Mary and John Gage, an officer of an Irish regiment stationed in the colonies. When James was four years old, his father was killed in battle, and his mother raised him and his sister, Elizabeth. In about 1790 May Gage brought her children into the Niagara region and settled in Stoney Creek near her brother, Augustus Jones.

In 1796, James married Mary Davis, who was born in North Carolina in 1777 and had immigrated to Canada with her family in 1794. James and Mary became well-known for their hospitality, providing a welcome stop for people travelling between York (Toronto) and Niagara, or from Niagara to the Grand River area. Opposite their home, James built a store, and he ran a very profitable business. He travelled often by boat between Stoney Creek and York, and was acquainted with and was well-liked by most people in this area, including Joseph Brant.

James and Mary had ten children, and in 1810 James purchased more than 300 acres of land in Wellington Square, now Burlington, from Catherine Brant. His sons settled there, and the area rapidly became a hub for shipping and lumbering. James was also a surveyor, and was the first to survey the village of Wellington Square. He was a member of the 2nd Flank company of the 5th Lincoln Militia, a volunteer company that received regular training in the event of an emergency.

During the War of 1812, when the American army set up camp in Stoney Creek, James and his family were imprisoned in the cellars of their home while the officers used it as their headquarters. Their home is now a museum, called Battlefield House in honour of the famous battle of June 1813. In 1835, James and Mary, along with his mother, moved to Hamilton, where he died in 1854.

Stella Clark

SIR JOHN MORISON GIBSON
(1842-1929)
Buried in Hamilton Cemetery, 777 York Boulevard, Section C3

When, in February 1892, Premier Oliver Mowat directed his Provincial Secretary to prepare child protection legislation for introduction in the current legislative session, John Gibson was taken aback. After much thought, he approached Mowat, requesting additional time for research and consultation. The premier agreed. Over the next year Gibson, ever the enthusiastic and thorough student, studied the problem of neglected and delinquent children. The legislation that he introduced in April 1893, the Children's Protection Act, forms the foundation for child welfare legislation in Ontario today.

John Gibson is one of the most remarkable and influential figures in Hamilton's history. A farm lad who showed academic brilliance early on, he shone at the University of Toronto where he studied "oriental languages" and the law. In a career that encompassed a thriving legal practice, military service, politics and business — he was a founder of the radial railway and electricity empire, Dominion Power and Transmission — and culminated in his appointment as Lieutenant-Governor of Ontario in 1908, Gibson was to view The Children's Charter as one of his most significant accomplishments.

As Ontario grew increasingly urbanized and industrialized through the last half of the 19th century, attention was drawn to the problem of neglected and delinquent children who were, many maintained, the criminals of tomorrow.

Earlier in the decade a Royal Commission had recommended the extension of the industrial school system under which these children were confined in an institutional setting. The Children's Charter, arguing that "prevention is better than cure," explicitly rejected this approach for one that was family-centred. The Act gave the courts power to sever parental relationships and to commit children to the guardianship of newly established

Children's Aid Societies, which would place them in foster homes. There, it was argued, they would be "well and properly cared for and given training for after life."

Family lore has Gibson personally delivering the first child placed in foster care under the Act to his new home. He attended and addressed meeting after meeting as local communities organized their own Children's Aid Societies. Together with his wife, herself an active social reformer, he continued to promote child welfare issues long after leaving active political life. It remained, he was to write in 1927, "a source of great satisfaction… that I had to do with the original legislation and work connected with child protection." Little could he have predicted that his legacy would endure today.

Carolyn Gray

JANE GILES
(1817-1915)
Buried in Grove Cemetery, Dundas, Single Section 14

Sometimes life does not work out according to plan. This was so for Jane Giles.

She was born Jane Smythe to an Irish family of considerable means. In 1838, at age 21, she set out for Toronto, having arranged to study as a teacher. A misunderstanding in travel arrangements found her instead in Ottawa, where she made her home.

In 1848 Jane moved to the United States where she met and married George Giles, a salesman and cutter in a tailoring establishment. They

Public and High Schools, Dundas, Ontario.

moved to Dundas in 1851, the voter's list naming George Giles as "school caretaker." Jane's life took a tragic turn with the death of George, victim of a scarlet fever epidemic.

Left with a daughter and two sons to support, Jane applied for the position of janitress of the Dundas Public School. It is one she would hold for 21 years. In 1879 her salary was $200, plus the use of a house on the southwest corner of the school grounds. The Dundas Public School Cash Book also lists extra payment for wood cutting. Jane became important in the lives of the students beyond the expectations of her role. As the children discovered her caring nature, she became "mother of the school." Her home was often a first aid establishment, where cuts, bruises and even broken bones were bound and the injured given tender loving care.

These kindnesses were not forgotten. When age made it impossible for her to continue working, Jane retired, moving to Chicago to live with her son. She missed Dundas, however, and was not content. Through the kindness of some Dundas friends she was brought back to reside in the House of Providence, until moving to the Ellen Osler Memorial Home in 1909 as one of its first residents.

Jane Giles died 12 March 1915, at the age of 98 years. Prominent citizens Lt. Col. H.C. Gwyn, S.N. Moffat, S.J. Lennard, Henry Bertram, Lt. Col. J.J. Grafton and W.A. Davidson served as her pallbearers. The newspaper reported,

> She was a woman beloved by all, and has exerted an influence for good with all she came in contact. The funeral was very largely attended, many who had come under her influence in earlier years being present to pay their last tribute of respect.

Embarking to Canada, 21-year-old Jane would never have imagined it.

Roberta Bailey
Carolyn Westoby

HENRY GOFF
(1857-1880)
Buried in Hamilton Cemetery, 777 York Boulevard,
Section Christ's Church Cathedral — D

On 3 February 1880, the mixed train to Collingwood left Hamilton at 9:00 a.m. and was running very late due to a snowstorm. Approximately a mile south of Glencairn, Ontario, one of the wheels of the locomotive broke, throwing it off the track and down an embankment. A young man named Henry Goff, a fireman, was instantly killed when the fuel tender jammed him against the boiler of the locomotive.

From the evening edition of the *Hamilton Spectator* dated 5 February 1880:

> An inquest was held on Wednesday afternoon at Lisle,
> Ontario in regard to the cause of death of fireman Goff
> killed on the Hamilton and Northwestern Railway the night
> before. The jury brought in the following verdict as follows:
>> Accident occurred by train leaving the track and
>> Goff being caught between the boiler of the
>> engine and the flat car. No blame was attached to
>> the company. Signed by Dr. Nesbitt, Coroner.

Henry Goff's mother was heartbroken at the news of her son. She left immediately for Glencairn to retrieve her son and brought his body home on the 11:30 a.m. train on Thursday. The funeral was to take place the following day at 3:00 p.m. from her mother's residence on Ferguson Avenue.

For her son, she erected a small headstone with a locomotive carved on the front and a wonderful poem inscribed on the back, which reads as follows:

> *My engine is now cold and still*
> *No water does my boiler fill*
> *My coal affords its flame no more*
> *My days of usefulness are o'er*
> *My wheels deny their running speed*
> *No more my guiding hand they heed*
> *My whistle too has lost its tone*
> *Its shrill and thrilling sounds are gone*
> *My valves are now thrown open wide*
> *My flanges all refuse to glide*
> *My clacks also, though once so strong*
> *Refuse to aid the busy throng*

No more I feel each surging breath
My steam is now condensed in death
Life's railway o'er each station past
In death I'm stopped and rest at last
Farewell all dear friends and cease to weep
In Christ I'm safe In Him I sleep

Paul Kuzyk U.E.

GREAT WESTERN RAILWAY CREW
DESJARDINS CANAL DISASTER (12 MAY 1857)
Buried in Hamilton Cemetery, 777 York Boulevard, Section A5 B5

Thursday 12 March 1857 — the afternoon train from Toronto, consisting of the locomotive *Oxford*, its tender, a baggage car and two first-class coaches, was due in Hamilton at 6:10 p.m. The train rounded the bay and approached Burlington Heights, where it would negotiate a switch and cross a 72-foot wooden swing bridge over the Desjardins Canal, covered with two feet of ice and 60 feet deep.

Travelling six miles per hour, it crossed over the switch and a sudden shudder like a thump went through the train as the front wheel of the engine broke, fracturing the leading wheel truck. Witnesses said the train started

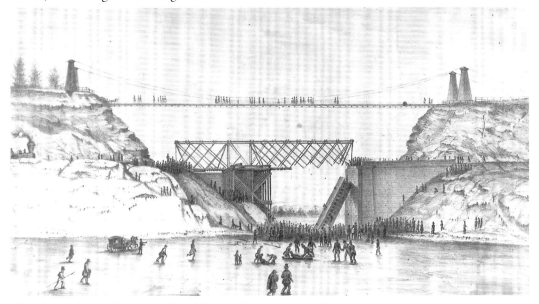

The aftermath of the Desjardins Canal disaster, showing rescue efforts.

swaying from side to side like it was coming off the rails. Engineer Alexander Burnfield immediately whistled for "on brakes." Failing to slow his train, he immediately tried to uncouple the train from the engine — to no avail. The crippled engine thumped its way over the railroad ties and onto the wooden swing bridge, its broken wheel crushing and splintering bridge supports until the deck finally gave way. The *Oxford* fell through the ice and the baggage car followed, falling to one side of the engine. The first passenger car flipped onto its roof and was badly crushed as it partially broke through the ice. The last car fell endways into the ice and remained nearly upright.

The news of the accident was known virtually within minutes. Rescue trains were dispatched and hundreds came from the city to help. Sixty people perished and almost all of the survivors were injured.

A makeshift morgue was set up in the freight shed of the Great Western Railway Station on Stuart Street. The morgue was quickly closed to the rush of onlookers and an artillery company formed a cordon around the room. Coroners assigned were Dr J.W. Rosebrugh and Harcourt Bull. They employed a new process for forensic identification: photography. Photographer Robert Milne was assigned to take pictures of the deceased.

An exhaustive investigation into the causes of the accident showed that the bridge was

> of sufficient strength for the conveyance of the traffic of
> the line safely and securely over said bridge, provided that
> the locomotive and cars remained on the railway track,
> but… was not built of sufficient strength to sustain an
> engine and train in case they should run off the track while
> passing over the said bridge.

However, Frederick P. Rubridge of the Department of Public Works produced samples of the bridge's wood rot that all other engineers overlooked, and declared the bridge was "virtually a catastrophe-in-waiting."

Railway workers erected a monument inscribed:

> *Alexander Burnfield lost his life while acting in his capacity as*
> *Engineer and George Knight lost his life while acting in his*
> *capacity as Fireman.*

A brass replica of the *Oxford* stood atop the monument until the Depression, when it disappeared, probably stolen and sold for brass content. Only a stone base is left atop the monument.

Paul Kuzyk U.E.

BILLY GREEN
(1794–1877)
Burial place unknown; monument in Stoney Creek Cemetery.

Billy Green, colourfully known as "the Scout," is Stoney Creek's answer to Laura Secord: a local boy who did great things in a pivotal moment of history.

Billy was born to Adam and Martha Green in 1794, one of the first children born to Loyalist émigrés in Saltfleet. His mother perished the same year, probably in childbirth, and Billy was raised by his father and his elder siblings. Life on a backwoods farm in the early 1800s was difficult, but the tightly knit Green family wrestled the rough land atop the escarpment into submission, forging a family farm around the intersection of Green Mountain Road and what is now Upper Centennial Parkway. This hamlet was once known as Greentown.

Billy Green's story goes largely unremarked in the official annals of the War of 1812. While the British surprise attack on the American encampment at Stoney Creek and the subsequent retreat of the invaders is noted as a decisive victory for the defence of Canada, Green's contribution remains primarily derived from his own writings in the 1870s.

Billy claims that as a mischievous 19-year-old, together with his brother Levi, he frightened the passing American troops that morning at Grimsby with native Indian war whoops.

Billy got the American password from his brother-in-law, Isaac Corman. The American officers had freed Corman because of his family connection to the American general William Henry Harrison. Green memorized the countersign and walked to the British encampment at Burlington Heights, on the far side of modern Hamilton. He then accompanied a detachment of British regulars east along King Street and, with the appropriate password, passed through the American pickets at the Red Hill Valley. The British forces surprised the American encampment, captured their artillery and sent the invaders back to the Forty (Grimsby) and eventually the frontier.

Green later inherited his father's farm, and around 1820 erected a red brick house that still stands on Ridge Road at Upper Centennial Parkway. Portions of the Green farm still survive as fruit-growing fields. Nearby Green Mountain Road is also named after the family.

Billy Green is commemorated in the Stoney Creek cemetery, but his resting place is unknown.

Michael Gemmell

A drawing of Hamilton's first courthouse, a log building originally at the corner of Main and John Streets.

GEORGE HAMILTON
(1787-1836)
Buried in Hamilton Cemetery, 777 York Boulevard, Section Z1

George Hamilton was a merchant in Queenston until, during the War of 1812, his home and business were burnt by the invading Americans. In 1815, he purchased 257 acres in Barton Township and moved to the Head-of-the-Lake.

While there, he went into an agreement with Nathaniel Hughson and James Durand to lobby the House of Assembly to have the new district courthouse and jail located on their land. Hamilton donated the land for the courthouse and divided the rest of his property into town lots. In 1827, the new expanding town site was granted the courthouse for the Gore District. Hamilton planned a market and named the streets after members of his family.

He died in 1836 and was buried in his family cemetery, located at the base of the Mountain access. In 1892, his and his family's remains were moved to the Hamilton Cemetery on York Boulevard. The city erected the family monument to honour not only the founder of the city of Hamilton, but the man who gave the city its name.

George Hamilton was a new radical entrepreneur, a British-American hybrid. His personal motto could have been, "for the public good, but for private profit" or, as in the movie, *Fields of Dreams*, "If you build it, they will come."

Donna Reid & Robin McKee

THOMAS WILLIAM HAND

(1868–1945)

Buried in Hamilton Cemetery, 777 York Boulevard, Section V

Son of Professor William Hand (1838–1901), T.W. Hand was trained by his father in the skills and artistry of pyrotechnology, or the creation of beauty and awe by the use of fireworks.

As early as 1875, Professor Hand had acquired substantial property on both sides of Hamilton's King Street West between Sophia (now Strathcona Avenue) and Dundurn Street. At first, there were just two small huts on the grounds used for the mixing of high explosives.

Even at the relatively youthful age of 14, small, lean and quick of movement, T.W. Hand took his abilities as an "artist in fire" on the road, setting off magnificent displays of coloured fire at a wide variety of special occasions all across the province of Ontario and beyond.

At the age of 20, T.W. Hand entered into partnership with Walter Teal and took the reins of his father's fireworks company. The King Street operations were expanded substantially with the addition of several more buildings. Vacant property farther to the west, in the location of the present Westdale neighbourhood, was purchased for the storage and testing of the Hand company's fireworks.

A major accident occurred at the Hand Company's King Street yards on 26 March 1900. Walter Teal and another worker were mixing explosives. Somehow an explosion occurred that shattered windows over a mile away. Both men were instantly killed.

The very next year, another tragedy took place at the King Street yards. On 11 October 1901, Professor William Hand himself was burned substantially in an explosion. He survived for a short time, but later died in hospital.

Despite the setbacks, T.W. Hand carried on with the fireworks business, eventually making it the biggest such company of its kind in Canada.

The Hand Company remained in Hamilton until 1930, when the Westdale testing area was sold for development, notably for the George R. Allan School and Westdale Secondary School.

Thomas William Hand remained in control of the company until his retirement.

One of Hamilton's most successful businessmen and colourful characters, Thomas William Hand died at the age of 77 and was buried in the Hamilton Cemetery.

J. Brian Henley

MATTHEW JOSEPH HAYES
(1894-1943)
Buried in Holy Sepulchre Cemetery, 600 Spring Gardens Road, Section N

Known as the Diamond Jim Brady of Canada, Matt Hayes took over the International House hotel on the northwest corner of James Street North and Barton Street, on the death of his father. Described by a contemporary as "full of pranks and inclined to corpulency," Matt was famous for his entertaining. He loved food and threw dinners at the Estaminet that were compared to Roman feasts. His lavish lifestyle included an expensive apartment over the Bank of Hamilton across from the hotel. It was not his income from the hotel, however, that financed his lifestyle. Matt's main source of revenue was his activities as a bookmaker. He was the bookie who would take on large bets that no one else could handle locally. He also took on heavy bets through the wire service from the United States. This was called the "hot wire stuff" and could be thousands of dollars bet on a hot nag at Pimlico or New Orleans.

Matt was very conscious of the plight of the northenders. He maintained a unique system of scouts who kept him constantly advised of any family who could not afford food or fuel during hard times. Any family in need would find a wagon full of coal or a food delivery turning up on their doorstep anonymously, although most knew the source was Matt.

Matt Hayes and friends.

Matt's weight reached 400 pounds and his doctor warned him that, unless he lost weight, he would be dead in two years. He remained a gambler to the end, refusing to abandon his love of food and his lavish style of living. Two years almost to the day after his doctor's prediction, Matt died at the age of 49.

Margaret Houghton

MARGARET JANET HAYWORTH
(1929-1939)

Buried in Woodland Cemetery, Spring Gardens Road, Section 25

On 3 September 1939, Canadians reached a pivotal point in their perception of the onset of World War II. Only two days after Hitler invaded Poland, the German submarine U-30, captained by Fritz-Julius Lemp, torpedoed the British Cunard transatlantic liner *Athenia*, 200 miles northwest of the Irish coast. The captain of the U-boat had mistaken the liner for a troop ship, as her portholes had been painted out and there were no lights visible. The torpedo hit the *Athenia* amidships and she was doomed. *Athenia* had been bound for Quebec and Montreal and carried, among its 1,418 passengers and crew, Mrs Hayworth and her two daughters, Margaret and Jacqueline, of Hamilton. Mrs Hayworth and Jacqueline survived the sinking of the ship, but Margaret was severely injured and was the first of 112 to die as a result of this enemy action.

This meant that Margaret was the first Canadian to die due to enemy action in World War II. Newspapers publicized the story for all it was worth, setting the tone for their coverage of the rest of the war.

The Athenia *under steam.*

One thousand people met the train that carried her body back to Hamilton, and there was a public funeral from St Andrew's Presbyterian Church. The mayor of Hamilton, William Morrison, and all of the city council attended, as did the Lieutenant-Governor, the Honourable Albert Edward Matthews, Premier Mitchell Hepburn, the entire Ontario cabinet and a military guard of honour.

Ironically, U-boat commander Lemp, who started the Battle of the Atlantic by sinking the *Athenia*, was also partially responsible for ending it. In May 1941, Lemp was in command of a new U-boat. During an attack on a convoy in the Baltic Sea, the British Navy attacked his submarine. Lemp escaped and is presumed to have drowned. But he made a serious mistake. He didn't scuttle his ship. The British boarded the U-boat and captured its Enigma machine. This secret German communications gear proved to be the Allies' key to stopping U-boats in the Atlantic.

Margaret Houghton

NORA FRANCES HENDERSON
(1900-1949)
Buried in Woodland Cemetery, Section 5W-1

Nora Frances Henderson began her working career as a reporter for the *Hamilton Herald* newspaper in 1918, becoming editor of the women's pages in 1921. She had always actively promoted the idea of women getting involved in politics and participating in the political life of Hamilton. She ran for alderman in Ward One in 1931 and won, becoming the first woman ever elected to Hamilton City Council. She served three terms. In 1934 she ran for a vacancy on the Board of Control, created when Sam Lawrence left to enter Ontario politics, and won, becoming the first woman elected to a board of control in Canada. She was subsequently re-elected 13 more times. She served on city council as alderman and controller for 16 consecutive terms. When Mayor Lawrence was out of town in June of 1946, she became the first woman to serve as acting mayor in Hamilton's history.

It was also in 1946 that Hamilton faced one of the largest labour strikes in its history, when the workers at the Hamilton Works of the Steel Company of Canada voted to strike on 23 May. They walked out to begin their strike on 15 July.

The City Council split in their attitude to the strike, with Mayor Lawrence and his supporters behind the strikers and Controller Henderson and her supporters opposed to what they referred to as the "city's state of

lawlessness." The picketing was, in fact, illegal and it was to that, among other issues, that Henderson objected. On 2 August she went to the plant and began a slow, lonely walk to the picket line. When she reached it, she demanded to be let in. The picketers stepped politely aside and let her in. When she left the plant she stated, "I will not bow to mob rule." She also called for a special Board of Control meeting to deal with the issue. Photographs of Nora Frances Henderson walking towards the picket line appeared in every major newspaper across Canada.

On 9 August the City Council met to consider the issue. Supporters of the office workers booed council members who were supporters of the strikers, and the strikers booed those who supported the office workers. After four hours of debate, the council voted nine to seven to not call in the Ontario Provincial Police. As councillors left the meeting they were booed or cheered depending on their stand on the issue. When Henderson appeared, the crowd of 2,000 became unruly and began to sing, "We'll hang Nora Frances from the sour apple tree." It was also reported "a man kicked her on the seat of her well-tailored suit." At one point it looked as if the crowd would overturn her car but, with police help, she was able to leave unmolested.

She retired from politics the following year to take over the position of executive secretary of the Children's Aid Societies of Ontario, and died two years later in 1949.

Margaret Houghton

GEORGE MUIR HENDRIE
(1865–1942)
Buried in Hamilton Cemetery, 777 York Boulevard, Section F2

George Muir Hendrie began his working career as a clerk in the Bank of Hamilton but, being a shrewd businessman, he found a way to combine his business acumen with his love of horse-racing. With his partner W.O. Palmer, he operated the Windsor Jockey Club track in Windsor. Under their management the track became the first in Canada to handle a million dollars in betting in a single day. When he stopped operating the track he focused his attention on racing and breeding thoroughbreds. He owned a breeding farm in Kentucky as well as a stock farm in Glanford Township, just outside Hamilton. His horse Springside won the King's Plate in 1918.

One of the best horses owned by Hendrie was Great Britain, winner of the 1913 and 1914 Toronto Autumn Cup at Woodbine Race Track. Great Britain proved to be one of the best long-distance racers of his years, winning distance races in the United States as well as Canada.

After being injured in a car accident, Hendrie retired from racing but continued breeding thoroughbreds at his farm in Glanford. For years he served as chairman of the Canadian Racing Association and, just before his death, was chosen president of the Ontario Jockey Club. K.R. Marshall, vice-president of the Ontario Jockey Club, issued the following tribute to Hendrie following his death:

> "It would be difficult to single out any other man in the entire history of Canadian racing who has done more to promote the best interests of the sport than Mr Hendrie.

He was a leading authority in all matters connected with the breeding and racing of thoroughbred horses and his death will be severely felt by a large circle of friends and associates."

Even in death his interest in racing was expressed. George Muir Hendrie is buried in the loving cup that his horse Great Britain won in 1914. The plaque over his grave reads:

> *A sporting son of a sporting father. A breeder and lover of thoroughbred horses, sporting dogs & game chickens. Buried in the "Louisville Cup" won by his horse "Great Britain" — 1914*

Margaret Houghton

JOHN HESLOP
(1812-1891)
Buried in St John's Anglican Church Cemetery, Ancaster

John Heslop was born in St Bee's, Cumberland, England, son of Robert and Diana Heslop. The family sailed from Scotland to New Brunswick in 1815. In 1817, they moved to Washington D.C., where they spent six years on a plantation four miles from the city. They later bought land near Bull Run, Virginia. However, by 1842 they bought land in Ancaster, Ontario, and about this time John married Elizabeth Aikman of Ancaster. They had one daughter, Sarah Ann, born 1845. Their farm was near Mineral Springs.

In 1851 Heslop became both the first reeve of Ancaster Township and the first warden of Wentworth County. In 1873, he was appointed clerk and treasurer.

In 1861, Heslop replaced his frame farmhouse with a more substantial one of stone. Woodend, as the house became known, was a large Gothic Revival building, set on top of a hill. Surrounding it were gardens laid out by the Hamilton landscape gardener George Laing. The house and grounds, both substantially altered, are now the headquarters of the Hamilton Conservation Authority.

Thieves broke into Woodend in January 1891, breaking down the back door with a cordwood stick, looking for the tax money that Heslop was rumoured to have in the house. Heslop was shot dead on the back staircase where, wielding a chair, he met the gunmen. No money was kept in the house, and the murderers left with a few trinkets. Although several men,

members of a gang, were tried for the murder, there was so much conflict-
ing evidence and so many alibis that they were found not guilty. The Heslop
murder was a sensation in Ancaster for many decades.

Not everyone was enamoured with John Heslop, however, and Alma Dick
Lauder gives an account of his death:

> John Heslop had a very large funeral having been a sort of
> public man in this neighbourhood… I counted 140 traps
> of different sorts… There are several morals to be deduced
> from this shocking affair. One is when you go out to meet
> a burglar take a six shooter instead of a chair and you will
> come off better… Another moral is don't lock your doors
> as they can always burst them in and it only… makes them
> angry and it is no use hearing them coming if you have no
> revolver. Also it proves that it is far better not to have a
> man in the house at all for if [the women] had been alone
> no one would have been hurt…

Paul Grimwood

Tombstones in the Hess Burying Ground.

MICHAEL HESS
(1740-1804)
Buried in the Hess Family Burial Plot, Mohawk Road West

Behind a church on Mohawk Road West, near Garth Avenue, is an abandoned
pioneer cemetery. The only forlorn headstone left is of Jane Snider, which
stands precariously on a small knoll, it and the others victims of vandals.

The site, surrounded by modern homes, is known as the Hess Cemetery.
This is a misnomer. Michael Hess, his wife Gertrude Charity and Jacob Hess
are the only Hess family members that are known to have been buried here.
The location has been given various other names, Terryberry and Hockley

Farm, but it lies on the property that belonged to Henry Smith.

In 1788, Michael Hess, Henry Smith, Aaron Kribs and William Rymal left their families in Pennsylvania and came to the Head-of-the-Lake, scouting out good farmland to resettle after the American Revolution. Michael Hess followed Chedoke Creek up the escarpment to find its source, for pure spring water. Here the men staked out plots of land, built shelters and then returned home to bring their families back the following year. By doing so, these families were the first settlers on Hamilton's Mountain.

In a fireplace, in the basement of the church on Mohawk Road, are three broken tombstones carefully stacked. They are the gravestones of Michael Hess, his wife Gertrude Charity (1744–1808) and Jacob Hess (1776–1823). Although badly cracked, with pieces missing, these stones were rescued from the cemetery, and the church is to be commended for trying to preserve this record of the past.

Donna Reid & Robin McKee

ADELAIDE SOPHIA (HUNTER) HOODLESS
(1858-1910)
Buried in Hamilton Cemetery, 777 York Boulevard,
Section Church of the Ascension — A

Adelaide Hunter Hoodless was a leading social reformer in 19th century Hamilton. It is believed her energy and determination was fuelled by personal tragedy.

In the rural community of St George, Hoodless witnessed the difficulties her widowed mother, with 13 children, faced in a society ruled by men. After her marriage to furniture manufacturer John Hoodless, Adelaide relocated

An early domestic education class in Hamilton.

to Hamilton. It was here, in 1889, that their infant son, Jack, died after ingesting infected milk.

Thus began Adelaide Hoodless' lifelong campaign to teach women the proper care of their children, their families and themselves. At the time, it was assumed that women required no such education. In 1893, Hoodless risked the ire of farmers' organizations when she stated publicly that they cared more for the welfare of their animals than the health of their wives and children.

By the late 19th century, Ontario adopted her education model. As one of the first women on the government's payroll, she travelled extensively to schools across the province.

Adelaide Hoodless was president of the Hamilton YWCA, first president of the National Council of the YWCA, one of the founders of the Victoria Order of Nurses and the National Council of Women, and creator of the Women's Institutes, which today have more than six million members worldwide.

The drive for domestic science education, which had expanded beyond cookery and sewing to include home management and scientific practices, required educated women to teach these skills to others. In 1900, Hoodless opened the Ontario Normal School of Domestic Science and Art in Hamilton. Twelve teachers graduated in 1903.

In 1901, desperate for money to keep the school open, Hoodless approached Montreal tobacco baron William Macdonald. As a supporter of education for women, Macdonald agreed to finance the Macdonald Institute to teach home economics, and the Macdonald Consolidated School to provide practice teaching facilities, both at the Ontario Agricultural College (now University of Guelph).

On the eve of her 53rd birthday, while speaking in Toronto, Adelaide Hoodless collapsed and died. In a life dedicated to public service, there is one

Eastcourt, the Hoodless residence, at Main and Blake Streets in 1899.

reference to her spontaneous, less serious side. Adelaide Hoodless was one of the first women to drive a car on Hamilton streets. On a plaque in the public school that bears her name, it mentions that she liked to drive fast. Perhaps it was because she had so many things to accomplish, and so little time.

Donna Reid & Robin McKee

LEWIS HORNING
(1775-1857)
Buried in Hamilton Cemetery, 777 York Boulevard,
Section Christ's Church Cathedral — B

Lewis Horning and his father Peter Horning came to Canada as United Empire Loyalists, settling in Hamilton in 1789. Young Lewis quickly established himself as a successful farmer, and by 1820 owned a general store, a grist and sawmill, and substantial land holdings all within Wentworth County.

On hunting in what was then Simcoe County, he became aware of an excellent milling site on the Pine River. In 1830 he purchased 2,500 acres in this area and planned his new community of Horning's Mills. That year he teamed the heavy mill machinery and supplies to Mono Mills, and from there he cut 26 miles of his own road so the wagon teams could pass. A dam was built with a 12-foot drop, as well as homes for all the workers and their families, and by 1835 Horning had established a self-sustaining community.

One day while getting ready to show some friends the best way home to Wentworth County, he was overheard saying he would give a dollar to find a lost cow and calf in the woods. Four children — two girls and a boy from the VanMear family, and nine-year-old Lewis Jr., — went into the woods to try and earn that dollar. After a long period of time, a search was conducted for the children, but all that was found was their footprints along with moccasin prints.

For two years the search went on for the missing children, including questioning all the local tribes, even trying to bribe one young man with $100 and Lewis' gold watch. After accepting the bribe, all the native man would tell him was, "You'll never find them," and "If I tell you, they'll kill me." One clue led them to Manitoulin Island but nothing was found. The VanMear boy, Oliver, showed up in a Toronto tavern, but no clues were forthcoming due to his mental illness.

Heartbroken, the Hornings returned to Wentworth County in 1838, never giving up hope of finding their lost son. Lewis died in 1857 while in the care of his daughter Susan Lottridge, leaving in his will a provision for his lost son, if ever he should be found.

Paul Kuzyk U.E.

OTTO IVES
(1801 OR 1804-1835)
Buried in St John's Cemetery, Ancaster

Otto Ives was the son of Edward Otto Ives of Bengal, in the service of the Honourable East India Company, and was a grandson of Edward Ives, an army surgeon who was with Clive in India. The family was extremely wealthy, and Otto was commissioned as a Cornet in the 7th Dragoons, a British Cavalry Regiment, in 1815, being placed on half-pay the following year. In 1819, he was commissioned as an Ensign in the 32nd Regiment of Foot, where he served until 1824. Ives spent some time in the Greek island of Cephalonia, and he married Magdalene, a Greek woman. One of their children, William Henry, was born in Corfu in 1833.

The Ives family came to Ancaster in 1833 and purchased the Hermitage from the heirs of George Sheed, Ancaster's first Presbyterian minister. They spent only two years there before Ives died in July 1835, and the family returned to England. His widow inherited his extensive property only as long as she lived in England or Upper Canada.

The Ives may have been a colourful family in the early days of Ancaster, but their contribution has extended to our own day. Mrs Ives and her sister, who accompanied her to Upper Canada, spoke only Greek. A young girl named Mary Rosebury was employed as a companion and teacher of English to them. Also in the household was a friend or relative of Mr Ives, who was so distressed at Mrs Ives' sister not returning his affections that he hanged himself on a tree in the bush. He is reported to be buried at the corner of the present Lover's Lane and Sulphur Springs Road, where his ghost is said to walk. However, this particular crossroads was not created until 1859, so if a suicide actually happened, the gentleman in question was not interred there.

Paul Grimwood

LYDIA ANN (SANFORD) JACKSON
(1804-1875)
Buried in Hamilton Cemetery, 777 York Boulevard, Section C4

Lydia Ann married Edward Jackson in 1826 and settled in Hamilton in 1830. Edward Jackson was a pioneer manufacturer in the metal business, producing stoves. Lydia Ann devoted herself to charitable activities.

Both worked to establish the Wesleyan Ladies' College, which opened in 1861. Housed in the Anglo-American Hotel on King Street East, the college

The Wesleyan Ladies' College, King Street East, now the site of the Royal Connaught Hotel.

attracted students from across Canada and the United States.

Lydia Ann worked to form the Ladies' Benevolent Society to help the sick and destitute. She was also involved in the construction of the Hamilton Orphan Asylum and its school.

Edward and Lydia Ann promoted the erection of Centenary Church in 1866. A memorial plaque in the church commemorates their good work.

The Jacksons resided on Maiden Lane, but after Edward's death, the city renamed the street Jackson Street to honour the man and his family.

Edward's property eventually passed down to his son-in-law, Senator W.E. Sanford. The mansion was known as Wesanford, a stately home that transformed the area into a fashionable centre of the city, known as Knob Hill.

Donna Reid & Robin McKee

GEORGE FREDERICK JELFS
(1853–1941)
Buried in Hamilton Cemetery, 777 York Boulevard, Section D4

On 12 July 1871, at the age of 18, George Jelfs arrived in Hamilton from England, and soon began to work in the office of prominent local lawyer R. F. Waddell.

After 20 years of distinguished work practising law in his adopted city, Jelfs was appointed a successor to Hamilton Police Magistrate James Cahill, who had served in that capacity for 30 years. George Jelfs would ultimately top that record of longevity.

Beginning on 22 May 1893, George Jelfs administered justice, dispensing judgments based on common sense and understanding rather than narrow judicial theories.

For the next 36 years of continuous service, Jelfs would ascend the bench of the Hamilton Police Court to deliver judgments to a daily succession of men and women charged with offences as relatively minor as public drunkenness to much more serious crimes.

On Jelfs' retirement from his position as Police Court Magistrate, the *Hamilton Spectator* noted that his " natural aptitude for his difficult office was combined with unimpeachable integrity. He has been a man of strong convictions and no sophistry or sentimentalism could sway him from what he believed to be the right judgment."

George Jelfs wrote and published five books: two on legal matters, three expressing his philosophy on life matters.

Most Sunday mornings, no matter what the weather, George Jelfs, a "fresh air fiend," was a familiar figure on the Hamilton streets, as he would walk from his home on Charlton Avenue West to the James Street steps, up the escarpment, along the Mountain brow to the Mount Hamilton Hospital and then back.

An ardent yachtsman and lawn bowler, Jelfs also took advantage of his

Judge Jelfs at work in his office.

community's beautiful location by owning a lovely summer home along the Beach Strip between Lake Ontario and the Hamilton Harbour.

George Jelfs died on 7 October 1941 in his 88th year, 12 years after his retirement from his Police Court duties.

His reputation as a dispenser and writer on justice matters had garnered Jelfs a national reputation. Locally, he was one of Hamilton's best-known public figures.

His funeral at Hamilton Cemetery was well attended.

J. Brian Henley

MAGGIE (CLARK) JOHNSON
(1841-1865)
Buried in the White Church Cemetery, Glanbrook
&
GEORGE WASHINGTON JOHNSON
(1839-1917)
Buried in Hamilton Cemetery, 777 York Boulevard, Section P

George Washington Johnson.

"When You And I Were Young, Maggie"

Although other countries have tried to claim this song and story as their own, it is a home-grown product of the 19th century, and it began and ended in the Hamilton area. Maggie Clark was born in Glanford Township, 14 July 1841, the eldest daughter of Joseph Clark and Elizabeth Bell. She attended a local school where, in her teens, her teacher was George Johnson, born in neighbouring Binbrook. Twenty-one-year-old George soon fell in love with his 18-year-old student and they spent many hours together sharing their love of music. A frequent walk took them to the banks of Twenty Creek where Maggie's father had a mill. It was here that George may have started his book of verses entitled *Maple Leaves*. One poem in it was called "When You And I Were Young, Maggie."

The young couple was soon engaged to be married, but there were serious health problems ahead for Maggie. She had contracted tuberculosis, which threatened their future. Each went their separate ways for higher education, but their love for each other did not diminish. On 21 October 1864, they were married in the Methodist church in Glanford.

George's career in journalism had led him to Buffalo, N.Y., and shortly thereafter to the *Plain Dealer* in Cleveland, Ohio. Tragedy struck the newly married couple when medical treatment failed to help Maggie and she passed away on 12 May 1865 at the age of 23, after less than a year of marriage. Maggie was buried in White Church cemetery, near Mount Hope, Glanford Township, a few short miles from where she was born. George resigned from his journalism post in Cleveland and returned home to Binbrook to become a teacher.

A year later, George asked a friend from Detroit, Michigan, J.C. Butterfield, to set music to "When You And I Were Young, Maggie." One of Maggie's sisters, Elizabeth Padgham, was the first person to sing the soon-to-become-famous ballad.

George taught public school in Binbrook, and Stoney Creek, and became principal of Hamilton's Central School in 1875. He later taught at Upper Canada College and was appointed a Professor of Language at his alma mater, the University of Toronto. His academic credits continued, as he was named Professor of Latin at Cornell University and received a degree of Doctor of Philosophy from Johns Hopkins University.

George died in 1917 while spending the winter in Pasadena, California. He is buried in Hamilton Cemetery and remembered by a monument erected in 1937 by the Hamilton Assembly of the Sons of Canada. The monument is a replica of a millstone opposite the west entrance to the Rock Gardens on York Boulevard, Hamilton.

Art French

ROBERT KIRKLAND KERNIGHAN
(1855-1926)
Buried in St Alban's the Martyr Anglican Church Cemetery, Rockton

In a corner of the churchyard of St Alban's Anglican Church at Rockton, Ontario, stands a cairn of field stone with a terse inscription in bold writing: *R.K. Kernighan "The Khan" 1855–1926.*

This monument, rough and wonderfully enduring, expresses the rugged strength of Robert Kirkland Kernighan, a bachelor, poet, journalist and rural philosopher. In today's society many would class him as an eccentric by both his appearance and actions. He was rather tall and quite slim. He had a very distinguished-looking nose and forehead. He always wore a white stiff collar and was partial to soft silk ties, especially red ones, which he wore tied in a huge bow. His sparse figure was covered with a long, flowing coat with velvet collar.

The Khan's writings were accepted by all who enjoyed his flair for describing the world around him — songs of the blackbirds in the swamps of Beverly, the voices of robins and warblers about his country home. His workshop, which he called the Wigwam, on the family farm Rushdale, was

the original log home of his grandfather. Vines grew prolifically over the house, covering the sides and doorway.

The birds found the vines an ideal place for nesting, and rather than disturb the nestlings, The Khan would climb into the Wigwam through a side window.

It was in 1891 that Sir John A. Macdonald enquired of him why he did not write a patriotic poem on Canada. The result was a masterpiece that years ago most Canadian school children knew by heart — "Men of the Northern Zone." It expressed The Khan's zeal for Canadian nationalism.

Robert Kirkland Kernighan died 26 November 1926. His funeral was in the little Anglican Church in Rockton, and most of his neighbours in attendance were in shock to see how many big, sleek city cars were there with representatives from the Toronto and Hamilton literary world, to pay tribute to this unique, perhaps eccentric, rural journalist.

Viola M. Collins

JOHN BENJAMIN BENSLEY
"BEN" KERR
(1884-1929)

Buried in Hamilton Cemetery, 777 York Boulevard,
Section Church of the Ascension — A

For entrepreneurial Canadians, Prohibition provided an ideal opportunity to get rich quickly by selling Canadian whisky and beer to the dry Americans at vastly inflated prices. The "great experiment," as Prohibition was called, came into effect in the United States on 16 January 1920. Legitimate Canadian distilleries expanded to supply the vast American market. They could legally export to the United States, but the United States could not legally import alcoholic beverages. That's where the bootleggers like Rocco Perri and Ben Kerr came into their own.

Bensley Kerr was born into a solid middle-class family. A tall, good-looking man with sandy blond hair and piercing blue eyes, Kerr dressed with elegance and style.

During and after World War I, Kerr worked as a plumber and a musician, as well as running a boat storage and rental business from his home at the foot of Bay Street North. After the war, his finances became perilous and the lucrative activity of bootlegging beckoned. He knew the lake well and owned a fast boat. By the middle of 1920 he had paid off his debts and was well on his way to being established as a bootlegger. By the spring of 1925 he was running three boats across Lake Ontario, regularly boasting, "I can outrun the feds any time."

Ben Kerr, the King of the Rumrunners, finally ran out of luck on 24 February 1929 when he and his associate set out to deliver a load of beer across the lake. They never arrived. On 29 March Kerr's body was found

Ben Kerr, seated on the left, beside his fiancée Louisa Byrens and her parents in 1911.

floating just off the coast of Lake Ontario near Colborne. The boat had split in the ice and the two men had been unable to reach shore.

His body was returned to Hamilton and, following a brief ceremony with only family, friends and police observers in attendance, Kerr was buried on 1 April 1929 in the family plot in Hamilton Cemetery. His name does not appear on the marker.

Margaret Houghton

ETHEL CAROLINE KINRADE
(1884-1909)
Buried in Hamilton Cemetery, 777 York Boulevard, Section M

Just before 4:00 p.m. on 25 February 1909 shots rang out, disturbing the quiet around 105 Herkimer Street. A woman ran screaming into the street proclaiming, "Ethel has been shot six times." The police were summoned and, on entering the house, found Ethel Kinrade dead of gunshot wounds. Her sister Florence, who had run out of the house, was hysterical. When the police were finally able to question Florence, her story was that a tramp had entered the house, demanded money and shot Ethel. Newspaper headlines sensationalized the search for the elusive tramp.

The inquest into the murder began on 10 March. Members of the family were called and testified that they did not know anything about the murder. Florence, when called to the stand, maintained her story of a tramp entering the house and shooting Ethel. It was pointed out that, although she had multiple opportunities to escape and call for help, she failed to do so. When asked for an explanation she was unable to give a plausible answer. It was also pointed out that the first bullets to Ethel's head were not fatal; the murderer would have had to reload and shoot her again, this time fatally in the heart at least 15 minutes later. When asked to explain this discrepancy in her story, Florence, who had been on the vaudeville stage, made a dramatic display of fainting on the witness stand.

The inquest concluded on 5 May 1909. The jurors' decision was that "the deceased met her death by gunshot wounds inflicted by some person or persons unknown to the jury." Florence and most of her family immediately left Hamilton, never to return. Ethel's murder is still officially listed as unsolved.

Speculation has always held that Florence was the killer, but no one will probably ever know for certain.

Margaret Houghton

The first Hamilton Public Library building on the north side of Main Street West at James Street.

RICHARD THOMAS LANCEFIELD
(1853–1911)
Buried in Hamilton Cemetery, 777 York Boulevard, Section O

In 1889 Richard Lancefield was hired as the first chief librarian of the newly formed Hamilton Public Library. He was well-known in literary circles as a bookseller as well as a passionate advocate for education and public libraries. He was described in the newspapers as popular and well-respected: "No man was ever better groomed by experience to fit into his life work." In the first ten years of his tenure at the library it became a model for public lending libraries.

Then, on 6 February 1902 Lancefield vanished from Hamilton. Before long the reason became obvious. The library board was notified by the Bank of Hamilton that there was a serious overdraft in the library's account. The total was found to be $5,000, or the equivalent to three years' pay for Richard Lancefield. Hamilton's chief librarian had developed a serious gambling problem and had been issuing duplicate cheques to cover his losses. He regularly frequented local poolrooms and placed bets on horses — usually long shots, usually losers. Just before he vanished he had also started investing in the stock market, usually picking stocks that immediately started declining in value. On the morning of 6 February, knowing that the bank could be stalled no longer, Lancefield went to the library. While there, between 6:00 and 9:00 a.m. he destroyed the minute books and other records that would have proved his embezzlement. He then boarded the train for Toronto and vanished.

The library's insurance carrier declined to cover the loss, maintaining that the board had not taken sufficient precautions. Lancefield's friends managed to come up with $1,700 towards the total loss and the library board declined to make any further claims, being embarrassed at the situation. The library by-laws were changed to ensure that the chief librarian and the treasurer of the library would not be the same person.

Lancefield never again set foot in Hamilton alive. Upon his death in 1911, however, his body was returned to the city for burial in the Hamilton Cemetery. Despite his shortcomings, Lancefield was responsible for laying the groundwork for an exceptional library system that is still in the forefront of library science in Canada today.

Margaret Houghton

ROBERT LAND
(ca 1738-1818)
Buried in Hamilton Cemetery, 777 York Boulevard,
Section Christ's Church Cathedral — C

In the old Christ Church Cathedral burial grounds of the Hamilton Cemetery stands a miniature Gothic-style chapel. Twenty-six Land family members are interred there, including one of Hamilton's earliest settlers, Robert Land.

Robert Land lived as a farmer in Pennsylvania and was a justice of the peace. At the outbreak of the American Revolution, he became a courier for the British, carrying dispatches between New York and the Niagara frontier. Both Land and his family suffered greatly at the hands of the rebels, who

A drawing of Robert Land's original cabin.

regarded him as a traitor and a spy for his pro-British activities. Family members were imprisoned, the family homestead was burned and his wife Phebe and their younger children were expelled to New Brunswick. Land himself was arrested twice and charged with being a British spy. He was found guilty and sentenced to death. General Washington ordered Land released on bail and Land escaped to Niagara.

Separated from his family, Land became one of the first settlers at the Head-of-the-Lake (Hamilton). In 1782 he was granted a 300-acre tract of land that extended from Burlington Bay to the Mountain and from present-day Wellington Street to Sherman Avenue.

Land hunted, trapped, fished and farmed the land. He is said to have grown the first wheat in the area.

In 1791, Land's wife and family, with whom Land had lost all contact, journeyed to Niagara. Hearing that a veteran bearing their name had recently settled at the Head-of-the-Lake they made their way there, hoping it was Robert. Miraculously they were reunited after nearly 12 years of separation.

When Robert and Phebe Land died they were interred in a small family burial ground near the cabin. In 1853 their son, Robert Land Jr., re-interred his parents in his newly constructed vault in the Hamilton Cemetery. The vault bears a United Empire Loyalist plaque denoting the family's status as British Loyalists.

Donna Reid & Robin McKee

FREDERICK AUSSEM LATSHAW
(1859-1944)
Buried in Grove Cemetery, Dundas, Oak Hill, Section 1

Keeping a diary during the Victorian era was an important pastime. At age 20, Fred Latshaw worked at his father Isaac's furniture store and funeral home on King Street in Dundas. These excerpts from Fred's diary relate a particularly heart-wrenching week.

Saturday, 25 October 1879 — Very foggy again today. Last night the mist was so thick that it drips off the trees. Mr. Marshall came in to buy a child's coffin. We are to make it tomorrow.

Sunday, 26 October 1879 — Went to the shop about 7:30 to finish the coffin. Mr. Jacob Bowman came in about 9 o'clock and got Pa to go with him as his father was dead. Pa went with him and I made the child's coffin, finished it at 1 o'clock. After dinner started lining Mr. Bowman's coffin and engraved the name plate. Later trimmed a coffin for a child of Mr. Pomfrets who died of diphtheria. Mr. Marshall's child died of diphtheria yesterday.

Tuesday, 28 October 1879 — Pa went to Mr. Bowman's funeral today. Made the shell for Mr. Pomfrets' coffin and took it to the cemetery in a wheelbarrow. At 4:00 went to Pomfrets' with the carriage, the funeral went to the church and then down to the cemetery. Drove the minister up to the rectory and came home for tea. It rained most of the time the funeral was going on.

Wednesday, 29 October 1879 — Worked in the shop today. Mr. Marshall came after dinner and wanted another coffin for one of his children, who had died of diphtheria, the second he has lost since last Saturday. Made the coffin and the shell and his boy took it out in our wheelbarrow.

Thursday, 30 October 1879 — We were woken up this morning about 5:30 by two men from Lynden who wanted a coffin for a child. Trimmed it and sent it off by 7:30 and then had breakfast.

Thoughts of death were never very far away from the minds of Victorians. Even the young would have experienced the death of friends and relatives many times. Despite the frequency with which one faced loss, the pain became no less intense. Fred Latshaw continued his father's business after Isaac's death in 1881, serving Dundas through the mourning traditions of the time until selling to W.L. Brown in 1912.

Carolyn Westoby

SAMUEL LAWRENCE
(1879-1959)
Buried in Hamilton Cemetery, 777 York Boulevard, Section Sunken Gardens

Each year thousands of Hamiltonians enjoy spectacular panoramic views, including awesome sunrises and sunsets, from Sam Lawrence Park overlooking the escarpment at Upper Wellington Street.

Sam Lawrence, tradesman, labour leader and politician, was indisputably Hamilton's "Mr Labour."

After World War II, industry and unions prepared to battle. Following a grinding depression and a devastating war, workers mobilized to demand a larger share of the economic pie. By the summer of 1946, stormy strikes were being waged in Hamilton at Stelco, Firestone, Westinghouse and the *Hamilton Spectator*.

The bitter 80-day Stelco strike in the summer of 1946 reflected the social schisms in our society and generated deep divisions within the community and within families.

Three thousand Stelco employees ignored the union's call for work stoppage solidarity and embedded themselves within the factories, determined to continue steel production. Confrontations between strikers and strike-breakers were frequent and often physical.

Stelco management and many citizens appealed to Mayor Sam Lawrence to call for extra police to protect strike-breakers who elected to cross the picket line. Lawrence, who had proclaimed at one rally that he was a labour man first and mayor second, refused.

Although city officials eventually called in police reinforcements, Lawrence's reputation as a totally committed pro-labour advocate was indelibly ensconced.

At one point, Sam's son Leonard headed the police department, which several times confronted pickets the elder Lawrence supported.

Although other Hamilton mayors adopted a pro-labour stance on occasion, Sam Lawrence was the only successful Hamilton mayoralty candidate

Samuel Lawrence, a pioneer of labour rights in Hamilton.

to run on a specifically pro-labour platform.

A less than stellar orator and writer, Sam's towering height and striking good looks, combined with a sincere demeanour, contributed to his electoral popularity. Trained as a stonecutter, Sam Lawrence served as union president, alderman, city controller, mayor and member of the provincial legislature. Although he never joined the Communist Party, Lawrence worked closely with left-wing radicals to improve the lot of workers. He campaigned for the eight-hour work day, unemployment insurance, national health insurance, old age security benefits and government ownership of important industries and utilities.

After his death in 1959, Sam Lawrence was eulogized by many who had opposed him. The *Hamilton Spectator*, a frequent critic, paid tribute to Sam Lawrence's integrity and dedication to the labour movement.

Ron Berenbaum

ERLAND LEE
(1864-1926)
Buried in Stoney Creek Cemetery

Erland Lee was from a prominent Saltfleet Township family. His father, Abram Lee, ran one of the most prosperous Stoney Creek Mountain farms from the 1860s on, and the well-connected family cultivated grapes and maple syrup as well as high-quality dairy products.

The Lee family was involved in local politics for three generations. Erland Lee was Township Clerk of Saltfleet for 20 years, drawing a modest $600 per year salary in 1917. He served on numerous agricultural boards and societies, but was especially associated with the South Wentworth Farmer's Institute, an education society for farmers dedicated to propagating scientific methods of agriculture.

It was his family connections that brought Erland Lee his primary fame: his key role in backing the 1897 formation of the Women's Institutes, the first rural women's organization. Somewhat paradoxically, the roots of this women's education society lie in the support of a man.

Erland was instrumental in not only suggesting the initial visit to Stoney Creek of Adelaide Hoodless, with whom the idea for the Women's Institutes germinated, but also in getting support from the men of his community, like federal politician E.D. Smith, and from the Ontario Department of Agriculture.

Erland Lee persuaded the male-dominated establishment to lend its moral, political and fiscal support to this pioneering women's group. His wife, Janet Lee, drafted the group's first constitution on the dining-room table of Edgemont (now Erland Lee Museum).

Erland Lee ran unsuccessfully for the provincial Conservatives in 1902. Alas, the Liberal candidate for South Wentworth, John Dickenson, carried the day. Erland Lee protested the election and asked for a recount. He lost the argument.

Erland Lee and E.D. Smith also jointly ran the Vinemount Creamery from 1899 to 1908. This shipping on the Toronto, Hamilton & Buffalo Railway for upper Stoney Creek's produce was also a processing plant for dairy goods from the Lee farm.

Given his background with womens' initiatives, it is amusing to note that in 1914, at a meeting of the Pinecrest Literary Society, Lee was put in the odd position of debating the negative side of the question: Should women be extended the franchise? To his credit, despite any personal qualms he won the debate.

Erland was quite close to his brother Marcus Lee, a Stoney Creek councillor around the turn of the 20th century. Marcus' only son, Harry Erland, was named for his uncle. Harry's 1916 death while serving in France in World War I, together with that of Erland's eldest son Gordon in 1917, hit the Lee family hard. While visiting Marcus in Hamilton in 1926, Erland Lee suffered a heart attack or stroke and died.

Michael Gemmell

JANET (CHISHOLM) LEE
(1862-1940)
Buried in Stoney Creek Cemetery

Janet Chisholm came from a prosperous Ancaster family. Her brother, James Chisholm, was prominent in forming Hamilton's Argyle and Sutherland Highlanders of Canada regiment.

Janet Lee was the fifth kindergarten teacher in Ontario, and introduced the kindergarten program to Hamilton in 1887 at Hamilton Central School. In 1987 the Hamilton-Wentworth School Board named a public school after Janet Lee on the 100th anniversary of the program's founding.

Janet was a lady of powerful personality. At the height of her teaching career, she was forced to cut it short by reason of marriage. Due to social pressures, married female teachers were not permitted. After 1890, Janet was forced into the societal role of the wife of a prominent farmer. This permitted her, however, great latitude in social work and she exercised considerable social influence.

Janet was the real instigator behind the organization of the Women's Institutes in 1897. Although the idea sprang from Adelaide Hoodless' call for women's education, and Janet's husband Erland supported the idea, it was Janet who personally brought the ladies of Saltfleet together. Janet had her husband drive her all over upper and lower Stoney Creek in the family's open horse-drawn cutter during the middle of February so that she could personally deliver invitations more than 100 local women. It was Janet who, after the initial meeting had gone so successfully, drafted the group's first constitution on her dining-room table.

It was Janet Lee who suggested that the membership dues for the Women's Institutes group be set at a very affordable 25 cents per year. This sum was well within the budget of a typical rural woman and was designed to make the new women's education society more inclusive.

Janet also attempted to set the tone of the group by proposing that each meeting of the Saltfleet Women's Institute be opened with a short recitation of the Lord's Prayer. This unifying Christian prayer was thought to put the ladies in a frame of mind suitable for education.

Janet suffered from the death of her eldest son, Gordon, in World War I, and from the relatively early death of Erland in 1926. Paralyzed by a stroke after 1930, she was bedridden in her home Edgemont (now Erland Lee Museum), until her passing in 1940.

Michael Gemmell

The Canadian Eclipse Expedition just prior to leaving for Labrador in 1905.

DANIEL BRAND MARSH
(1858-1933)
Buried in Hamilton Cemetery, 777 York Boulevard, Section M

From his earliest days on a farm in Gray County, Daniel Marsh showed a distinct scientific aptitude. He built machinery from spare parts and apprenticed to both a watchmaker and a cabinet-maker. Other interests prevailed, however, and he graduated from the University of Toronto in 1888 and went on to attend Knox College. After graduation he was ordained a Presbyterian minister and later went on to earn postgraduate degrees in the United States. All his university studies were financed by his watchmaking ability. He served parishes all over Ontario and as far afield as Hamilton, Bermuda. It was during his tenure in Hamilton, Ontario, however, that his true passion was unleashed. Marsh, according to the *Dictionary of Hamilton Biography*, "inherited a love for the night skies from his mother, who gave him his first lessons in astronomy." With his scientific curiosity aroused, he began to experiment with astronomy and how the science of optics and photography could be applied to the study of the heavens. This interest resulted in the formation of the Hamilton Astronomical Society on 10 December 1901.

In 1905, Marsh was part of the Canadian Eclipse Expedition to Labrador, one of the four participants representing the Royal Astronomical Society of Canada. Also represented were the Dominion Observatory at Ottawa and the Royal Observatory at Greenwich, England. The expedition was under the leadership of John Stanley Plaskett (1865–1941) of the Dominion Observatory in Ottawa, the father of modern astronomy in Canada. Plaskett was particularly interested in the use of photography in astronomy, as was Marsh. They set out by ship for Labrador and built their eclipse camp. The eclipse of the sun at Domino, Labrador, began 30 August at 6:51 a.m., reached totality at 7:54 and 10 seconds and lasted 2 minutes and 38 seconds. The eclipse ended at 9:40 a.m. Plaskett, Marsh and other photographers photographed the entire expedition, from start to finish.

Marsh died at Hamilton, on 22 September 1933 and is buried in the Hamilton Cemetery. His tombstone has a plaque with an illustration of a telescope on it.

Margaret Houghton

JAMES MARSHALL
(1852-1929)
Buried Barton Stone United Church, 21 Stone Church Road West

James Marshall was born in a log house on his father's farm in Barton Township, above the escarpment, on 27 April 1852. He was educated in a school on the Mountain and later in the Hamilton Collegiate Institute. He followed farming as a life occupation, but had other interests as well — politics and cycling.

Prominent in township and county political affairs, Marshall served four years as assessor, served three years as auditor and spent time as a Barton Township councillor and deputy reeve. He became reeve of Barton and was Warden of Wentworth County in 1900.

He was a lifelong abstainer from liquor and tobacco, believing that this aided in keeping himself fit. His ideas of personal health extended to refusing to wear heavy clothing in the winter, never appearing in an overcoat.

James Marshall became famous throughout this section of Ontario for his wonderful physical vigour, which continued unimpaired after he had passed the allotted span of three score years and ten. During his lifetime he travelled by bicycle a distance of well over 100,000 miles, and at the age of 74 thought nothing of riding 100 miles a day or pedalling up the Jolley Cut, a feat he declared he could perform without losing breath.

From 1895 to 1926, he made journeys that averaged 5,000 miles every

The Jolley Cut road down the Mountain, Hamilton, Ontario.

year. The longest trip he ever made was to Brandon, Manitoba, every mile of which was accomplished on foot or on his bicycle, with the exception of ferrying across two rivers. Other trips carried him to all parts of Ontario in all kinds of weather.

Mr Marshall, even when a man of mature years, had powers which would have been envied by many an athlete. In a little book he kept the timetable of all his wanderings. One entry for the year 1903 is eloquent:

> Left Hamilton at five minutes to 5 a.m. Passed Brantford
> at 6:45 a.m. Stopped for an hour by the way to visit rela-
> tives. Reached London at one o'clock p.m. Reached Sarnia
> at 8 p.m.

He averaged about twelve miles an hour on his trip.

He died 1 October 1929, on the same farm where he was born, and was buried nearby in the cemetery of Barton Stone United Church.

Art French

MICHAEL MCCONNELL
(1838-1876)
Buried on the grounds of the Barton Street Jail, Barton Street East

On 5 January 1876, Nelson Mills was attacked and stabbed beside his home at the corner of King and Queen Streets by market butcher Michael McConnell. Mills had attached McConnell's goods for non-payment of rent. McConnell had been withholding the rent ($14) to try to force the landlord to make some much-needed repairs. When Mills continued to press to evict him, McConnell had calmly taken his knife and left the market to confront him. He stabbed Mills eight times. Nelson Mills died four days later on 9 January 1876, after an attack of hiccups had caused an inflammation of the wound and weakened him fatally.

By 7:30 that evening a jury had been sworn in and had gathered at Palm's Saloon at the corner of King and Bay Streets. They examined the body at the home of the victim and listened to eyewitness accounts of the crime. The coroner's jury found cause to send McConnell to court on a charge of murder.

John Crerar defended him using the plea of not guilty by reason of insanity, the first time this defence had been attempted in Canada. Crerar called several expert witnesses who testified that McConnell had previously suffered a severe blow to the head, which affected his ability to reason in support of this defence. McConnell always maintained that he was not responsible, that it was his passion that did it. Nonetheless, he was found guilty and sentenced to death.

An illustration of Michael McConnell's assault on Nelson Mills.

The *Hamilton Spectator* reported that on the morning of 14 March 1876, Michael McConnell "paid the penalty of his terrible deed with forfeiture of his life upon the scaffold. Even up to the last, he manifested nothing, which could be called penitence for his crime. The same perverse theory which he put forward in his first defense he clung to to the end." After the hanging McConnell became the first executed prisoner buried in the yard of the newly opened Barton Street Jail.

Margaret Houghton

JOHN V. MCGOVERN, V.C.
(1825-1888)
Buried at Holy Sepulchre Cemetery, 600 Spring Gardens Road, Section E

John McGovern was born in Ireland. In 1846 he arrived in India and was posted to the First European Bengal Fusiliers.

John McGovern, in a tough regiment, was one of the toughest. On 23 June 1857, he performed many acts of valour — one of which was to rescue a wounded comrade lying within yards of one of the enemy's gun batteries. McGovern ran forward, paused to make a rude gesture towards the enemy gunners, heaved the wounded man across his shoulders, paused again to shout to the enemy gunners what he thought of their shooting, then ran back, amidst a hail of fire from the outraged mutineers.

Two acts of outstanding bravery followed during the same campaign. Two years earlier a special medal had been created for acts of bravery, and McGovern became one of the first men to receive the Victoria Cross, recommended for all three actions where he showed outstanding bravery.

After his military service he returned to Ireland, married and immigrated to Canada, settling in Hamilton in 1863. He went to work on the docks.

Legend has it that during the vice regal visit of the Governor-General the Marquis of Lorne and his consort Princess Louise in 1879, McGovern had another foray into the limelight. He dressed up in his best, including his medal, and carrying his swagger stick went off to the Crystal Palace to greet the vice regal couple. As the couple passed, McGovern leaped to attention and saluted smartly, using his cane as if it were a sword. Recognizing the "tuppennyworth of bronze," as the Victoria Cross was known colloquially, the vice regal couple stopped immediately to greet McGovern as the hero that he was.

In later years he became a messenger for the customs service in Hamilton and would regale his fellow workers with stories, such as the one in which he rescued his officer, who had been treed by a tiger, by the simple expedient action of walking up and shooting the tiger with his Enfield rifle. After his death, McGovern's medals were sold for £80 to the Munster Regiment.

Margaret Houghton

DR JOHN OWEN MCGREGOR
(1850-1928)

Buried in the McGregor Plot, Union Cemetery, Margaret Street, Waterdown.

The inscription on Dr John Owen McGregor's monument in Union Cemetery reflects his place in Waterdown's history, but the epitaph, which reads, "Administered to the sick in this district for 48 years," tells only a small part of this village doctor's life.

John Owen McGregor was the second son of a successful Nelson Township farmer. He attended the University of Michigan at Ann Arbor, where he obtained his medical degree in 1873. On returning to Canada, he enrolled in further medical studies at the University of Toronto and,

Dr. John Owen McGregor and family.

following graduation in 1875, he moved to Dundas and set up his first medical practice.

A decade later he moved to Waterdown, locating his practice in a building on the southeast corner of Dundas and Main Streets, where he also operated a pharmacy. He acted as both physician and druggist, prescribing and filling prescriptions. In later years, his interests included archaeology and politics but, to the inhabitants of Waterdown and East Flamborough, Dr McGregor is remembered for his devotion to medicine and the welfare of the community.

An article in the *Hamilton Spectator* on 16 January 1892, commenting on the spread of grippe (influenza) in the countryside, stated "Dr. McGregor of Waterdown has ninety-one patients sick with him. He drives nearly 100 miles a day between 7 a.m. and 9 p.m., using up two teams of horses. Some nights he does not get to bed at all." He made home visits in Waterdown for 50 cents, and his charge for confinements was five dollars. The day after a medical visit he always made a courtesy call, often accompanied by his wife. He was described as "a venerable old type country physician" and "a law unto himself."

In late November 1927, Dr McGregor was hit by a motor car and, as a result of his injuries, was forced to end his medical career. He died in the Hamilton General Hospital on 23 April 1928 from complications resulting from the accident. An editorial in the *Spectator* later in the week noted his passing:

> He was more than the family physician, he was the family
> adviser and mentor, friend and guide; he was loved and
> trusted by all, even by those who came under the lash of
> his honest candour and outspoken admonitions.

Sylvia Wray

THOMAS G. MCILWRAITH
(1824-1903)
Buried in Hamilton Cemetery, 777 York Boulevard, Section R

In 1853, at the age of 29, Thomas McIlwraith emigrated from his native Scotland to Hamilton, where he took up employment as manager of the Hamilton Gas Works.

One of the city's leading businessmen of his day, McIlwraith served on several boards in the banking and insurance fields. But it was his passionate interest in the native birds of Ontario that led to his most lasting legacy.

Whether deliberate or not, McIlwraith's choice of the Hamilton area was inspired. The variety of habitats locally and the area's location on major migration routes meant that a huge number of bird species could be recorded within a short distance of his home, Cainbrae, at 503 MacNab Street North. Whatever the weather or time of the year, Thomas McIlwraith was a familiar figure walking along the bay shore, to Coote's Paradise and along the Niagara Escarpment searching for bird specimens.

As was the custom of the day, McIlwraith was less a bird-watcher than a bird-hunter. His goal was to kill the interesting bird species he encountered, so that he could make detailed records of weight, plumage and other factors. Eventually, using his considerable taxidermy skills, he would stuff and mount many of the specimens.

In 1860 McIlwraith published a list of Canadian bird species in the *Canadian Journal*. Containing the names and descriptions of 202 species, that list was one of the first comprehensive surveys in Canadian ornithological history.

In 1886, the Hamilton Association published McIlwraith's *Birds of Ontario*, the first such detailed description of Canadian birds. Besides scientific descriptions of each bird, McIlwraith added a paragraph or two about where and when he first saw that particular species. Most of the descriptions had specific Hamilton-area references. Seven years later, *Birds of Ontario* was updated and republished with a distribution all across the province.

Upon McIlwraith's death in 1903, the *Hamilton Spectator* noted that "no man knew more of the Birds of Ontario than he, and he was recognized everywhere as the highest authority."

J. Brian Henley

WILLIAM MCKINLAY
(1807–1849)
Buried in West Flamborough Presbyterian Church,
Highway #8, West Flamborough Township.

Credit for the early industrial development of the Flamboro Stream, or Spencer Creek, is largely attributed to the foresight, ambition and investment of West Flamborough entrepreneur James Crooks. However, there were others who also saw the potential power the stream provided and established industries that brought prosperity to the township during the first half of the 19th century. Among them was a young, ambitious industrialist named William McKinlay from New York State, who came to the township in 1828.

McKinlay described himself as an iron founder at the time of his marriage to a member of the Van Every family; shortly afterwards, he purchased an acre of Lot 3 Concession 2 in the township and erected an iron and brass foundry. For many years this was the only one in the surrounding farming area, manufacturing such necessities as stoves, gears, steam engines and agricultural implements. On 26 February 1846, William McKinlay was the first West Flamborough resident to be awarded a patent for an invention, #209 for "An improvement in Horse-Threshing Machines." Later in the same year, the November issue of the *Ontario Farmer's Magazine* reported that McKinlay had sold 135 threshing machines in 1845 and "had begun to manufacture separators that could be applied to any horse power."

Although McKinlay was a truly successful manufacturer and his foundry provided employment to the area during the 1830s and 1840s, William and his wife Elizabeth had tremendous personal sadness in their lives. Ten children were born to the couple between 1833 and 1848, but only four survived to adulthood, a result of the many fatal childhood diseases prevalent in rural areas where there were so few doctors.

On 8 August 1849, at the age of only 42 years, William McKinlay died and was buried in the Presbyterian Church Cemetery alongside several of his children.

Sylvia Wray

MACNAB FAMILY

Re-interred in Hamilton Cemetery in May of 1909,
777 York Boulevard, Section M

At the far east end of Dundurn Park, near the corner of Tecumseh and Inchbury Streets, there once existed a private walled cemetery. Sir Allan Napier MacNab had set up Inchbuie, named after the ancestral burial ground of the MacNab clan in Scotland, during the 1830s when his only son, Robert, was killed in a shooting accident. Robert MacNab was the first of several burials in the enclosed graveyard.

MacNab also brought the bodies of his parents, Allan and Anne MacNab, and his first wife, Elizabeth Brooke MacNab, from their original burial places and re-interred them there. Later interments included his second wife, Mary Stuart MacNab; his brother David Archibald MacNab and two of David's children who died in infancy; and MacNab's daughter Minnie MacNab Daly. In 1862, following his death, Sir Allan MacNab's own remains were buried at Inchbuie.

The estate went out of the hands of the MacNab family, with the exception of the plot of land containing Inchbuie. Mrs French, a descendant of the MacNabs, entered into talks with the city of Hamilton to try to transfer ownership of the property to the city.

In 1909, after prolonged negotiations with the City of Hamilton failed, she sold the plot of land to a developer who was intending to use the land as a gravel pit. In May of that year, the bodies were disinterred and removed from Inchbuie. Sir Allan MacNab and the family of his second marriage, who were Catholics, were all re-interred at Holy Sepulchre Cemetery. The rest of the family, being Anglican, were buried in Hamilton Cemetery.

In 1967 the Canadian Club erected a monument to Sir Allan MacNab in Holy Sepulchre Cemetery. The graves of the other MacNabs resting in Hamilton Cemetery, however, remained unmarked. Interred there are Allan & Anne MacNab (parents), Elizabeth Brooke MacNab (first wife), Robert MacNab (son), David Archibald MacNab (brother), Napier MacNab (nephew) and David Archibald MacNab Jr (nephew). In May of 2004, the Head-of-the-Lake Historical Society will unveil a monument to these MacNabs, finally marking their final burial place after almost a century.

Margaret Houghton

MARY JANE (BAKER) MCQUESTEN
(1849-1934)

Buried in Hamilton Cemetery, 777 York Boulevard, Section D5

Mary Jane Baker McQuesten is recognized as the domineering matriarch of the McQuesten family. The death of her husband, Isaac, when she was only 39 left her to raise six children — four girls and two boys — on her own. Although she was accustomed to an affluent life in the family home, Whitehern, poor investments and drinking had all but wiped out family fortunes by the time of Isaac's death. McQuesten managed to maintain her family's standing in the community and survived financially through the kindness of family friends. They lived in a state of genteel poverty. Mary McQuesten controlled her children and made decisions for them until her death.

The other mantle she wore was that of influential feminist and social reformer. She used her membership in the MacNab Street Presbyterian Church to initiate change and challenge the male-dominated hierarchy of the church. With incredible fortitude, McQuesten mustered the energy and resolve to strive for social reform. She helped create the Women's Missionary Society in Hamilton and later worked to establish the Women's Foreign Missionary Society (WFMS). For more than 25 years she served on

The McQuesten family (left to right): Hilda, Thomas, Mary Baker McQuesten, Edna, Ruby, Calvin and Mary at the rear.

the executive of the local chapter of the WFMS. Her Christian zeal, organizational skills and command of the English language made her a dynamic and effective lecturer and leader.

Through her involvement with the National Council of Women, in 1889 McQuesten helped create the Hamilton chapter of the YWCA. She feared an increase of moral degradation with the influx of unskilled women workers for the rapidly expanding factories throughout the city. McQuesten focused on the Christian and moral aspects of the organization, sometimes at odds with Adelaide Hoodless who focused on the education and teaching of domestic science at the YWCA.

A prolific writer, her many remaining letters document a life of social responsibility and an unerring dedication to her church, community and family.

Donna Reid & Robin McKee

THOMAS BAKER
MCQUESTEN
(1882-1948)
Buried in Hamilton Cemetery, 777 York Boulevard, Section D5

Much of the natural beauty and green space in urban Hamilton today can be directly or indirectly credited to the work of Thomas B. McQuesten.

McQuesten was born in Hespeler, Ontario, on 30 June 1882, and was one

Thomas Baker McQuesten.

A postcard image of a section of the world-famous Rock Garden at the Royal Botanical Gardens.

of six children in the McQuesten family to survive to adulthood. While living at Whitehern, Thomas lost his father at the age of five. He attended University College at the University of Toronto, entered law school at Osgoode Hall and was called to the bar in June of 1907.

McQuesten entered local politics in 1913, successfully landing a seat on city council. He served as councillor for seven years, before being appointed to Hamilton's Board of Parks Management. As a member and chair of the parks board, Thomas spearheaded and oversaw the purchasing and development of more than 2,500 acres of parkland in the Hamilton area. Among the parks developed under his leadership were Gage Park, Mountainside Park, the Civic Golf Club, Scott Park and Inch Park. He was also instrumental in the beautification of the Niagara Escarpment through plantings along the escarpment face in Hamilton.

Thomas played a principal role in the improvement of Hamilton's western entranceway. The current high-level bridge on York Street and the Rock Garden (reclaimed from an open quarry pit) were the crowning achievements of an advanced redesign of the (then-called) Toronto–Hamilton Highway. Through McQuesten's skilled leadership, the new western entranceway was completed during the Depression years and helped to keep many Hamilton workers employed.

However, McQuesten's most lasting legacy is found in two of Hamilton's best-known institutions, McMaster University and the Royal Botanical Gardens. Thomas was instrumental in bringing McMaster University to the West Hamilton area, through creative use of park-board funding and parkland donation. Through McQuesten's work, the Baptist-based university was able to maintain its important separation between church and state as it moved to its new location.

A tour of botanical gardens in England and Scotland in 1924 gave McQuesten inspiration to develop a botanical garden in Hamilton. By associating the new gardens with McMaster University to permit the use of the term "Royal," McQuesten was able to preserve a large area of Cootes' Paradise and create a world-class botanical garden, conservation area and bird sanctuary.

Marnie Burgess & Spencer Snowling

JOHN MOODIE JR
(1859-1944)
Buried in Hamilton Cemetery, 777 York Boulevard, Section Z

The son of prominent businessman John Moodie, one of the Five Johns of Cataract Power fame, John Jr was assured wealth and social prominence from birth. He did, however, have his own successes in business. He invested heavily in his father's power company, with significant returns, and later assumed presidencies of Royal Distillery and Robinson Industries.

John Moodie Jr is best remembered for his obsession with new and modern modes of transportation. In 1878 he imported the first bicycle to Canada from Great Britain. He drove his penny-farthing on the streets of Hamilton for his own amusement. Newly enthralled with two-wheel transportation, he then brought the first low-rise bicycle to Hamilton. He rode in the first bi-

James Moodie driving his father's Winton, Hamilton's first car.

cycle race ever held, at the Canadian National Exhibition in 1881.

In 1898, he imported a Winton automobile from Cincinnati. The first car in Hamilton was also the first gasoline-powered car in Canada, the second in North America. This began John Moodie Jr's lifelong affair with the automobile. On 12 April 1898, Moodie gathered 19 men, with ten cars between them, to create the Hamilton Automobile Club. This organization, the first of its kind in Canada, exists today as the Canadian Automobile Association (CAA).

Part of the group's mandate was to make car travel both safer and more enjoyable. They drafted the first rules of the road, determined speed limits, posted directional signs and patched ruts. They promoted automobiles as a safer, cleaner alternative to horse-drawn vehicles. Little did they imagine the impact the automobile would have on future generations.

On occasion, Moodie opted for water transportation. In his lifetime he crossed the Atlantic Ocean more than 50 times. He is also credited with having the first motorboat on Burlington Bay. Later in life he supervised the construction in England of a turbine steamer. In 1904, when this ship arrived in Hamilton, it was named the *SS Turbinia* and became the first steamer on the Hamilton–Toronto run.

When he died at age 85, Moodie was still a member of the Hamilton Automobile Club.

Donna Reid & Robin McKee

LUKE MULLOCK
(1806–1893)
Buried in Grace Anglican Churchyard, Mill Street North, Waterdown.

Luke Mullock was born into the family of a wealthy shipbroker and general commission merchant from Limerick, Ireland. Not affected by the terrible conditions in Ireland during the famine years of the 1840s, Luke Mullock, his wife and three children sailed for Canada in one of his father's ships, the *Jane Black* on 24 July 1846, their youngest son dying during the six-week voyage.

The family lived in Hamilton for a few months before moving to property on the edge of the Niagara Escarpment, just west of the village of Waterdown. Throughout his life in Canada, Luke Mullock appears to have been a man of independent means, his occupations being listed in the various Wentworth County Directories of the 1860s and 1870s as a gentleman and farmer. He was also a portrait and landscape painter of some note, and several of his water-colours are still in local ownership. However, his name in the Waterdown area is synonymous with his interest in local archaeology

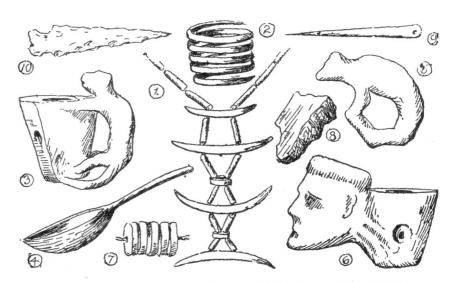

THE LATE LUKE MULLOCK'S COLLECTION OF MEDAL RELICS.

1—Conch shell and red pipestone necklace.
2—Copper finger ring.
3 and 6—Totem pipes.
4—Highly polished bone spoon, five inches.

5—Totem.
7—White wampum beads.
8—Paint stone.
9—Bone needle, five inches.
10—Flint arrow head.

and the collecting of First Nations' artefacts.

During the last 25 years of Mullock's life, this developed into a passion that he, together with his Waterdown friends Dr John Owen McGregor and George Allison, conducted at the nearby Lake Medad area. The site had been home to the Mississauga Indians during the 18th century. Before this a Neutral Indian village had existed along the shores of the lake for at least 700 years prior to their decimation by the Iroquois during the middle of the 17th century.

Many of Luke Mullock's finds were outstanding in their quality and uniqueness. The collection, that numbered several hundred pieces, included shell, glass, bone and stone beads, stone and ceramic pipes, iron axes, necklaces, antler harpoons and turtle-shell rattles.

Following his death in 1893, the collection was acquired by Dr McGregor, who chose to sell it into private ownership. George Allison's collection went to the Royal Ontario Museum in Toronto. The Mullock collection surfaced in the United States and was eventually purchased by well-to-do engineer and banker, George Gustav Heye, founder of the Museum of the American Indian Heye Foundation that was established in New York City in 1916. In 1990, the Heye Collection was incorporated into the Smithsonian Institute in Washington, D.C.

Sylvia Wray

DR ALFRED PAIN
(1888–1912)
Memorial in Hamilton Cemetery, 777 York Boulevard, Section W

On the night of 14 April 1912, the White Star's royal mail ship *Titanic* struck an iceberg and sank in the frigid waters of the North Atlantic Ocean. More than a thousand men, women and children lost their lives that night, among them Hamilton resident Dr Alfred Pain.

After attending postgraduate medical courses in England, Pain was returning home to Hamilton. He and the other passengers must have thought it a privilege and an adventure to be on the maiden voyage of the pride of White Star's fleet. Nobody could imagine what their fate would be. No marine disaster has touched the psyche of the world more than the sinking of the unsinkable *Titanic*.

A romantic story emerged from the disaster. Alfred Pain, through a mutual friend, looked up a Miss Marion Wright on board the *Titanic* and promised that she would be his charge during the crossing. His last known act was to put her into a lifeboat. He took her out of the crowd on one side of the ship and made sure she was in a lifeboat on the other side, saving her life.

Dr Alfred Pain, known as "Alf" by his friends and family, was lost at sea. His family plaqued the family headstone, marking the lot in his memory. The plaque reads,

> *Sacred to the memory of ALFRED PAIN, M.B., beloved son of Albert and Fanny Pain. A passenger on the ill-fated Titanic, which sank at sea on April 15ᵗʰ, 1912. Aged 24 years. "Safe in the arms of Jesus"*

Alfred Pain was only 24 years old when disaster struck, and both he and the ship went down in history.

Donna Reid & Robin McKee

Crowds gathering outside 166 Bay Street South for Bessie Perri's funeral.

BESHA "BESSIE" (STARKMAN) TOBIN PERRI
(1890-1930)
Buried in the Ohev Zedek Cemetery, west side of Upper James Street just south of Limeridge Road

In August of 1930 Hamilton was eagerly anticipating the start of the first British Empire Games. But it was another event that occurred on the evening of 13 August that focused attention away from the Games.

Local bootlegger Rocco Perri and his common-law wife Bessie were returning to their home at 166 Bay Street South at about 11:15 p.m. Suddenly, shots rang out and Bessie Perri lay dead in a pool of blood. Rocco ran out of the garage shouting, "My girl has been shot." Police recovered two 12-gauge, double-barrelled rifles, wiped clean of fingerprints, near the scene. Although the getaway car was later located, no one was ever arrested for the murder.

Bessie had been the financial brains behind Perri. Between the two of them, they ran the illicit liquor trade in Hamilton, collecting not a few enemies along the way.

At first, no rabbi would agree to officiate at Bessie's funeral. However, Rocco managed to find a rabbi and secured, for $2,000, a plot in Ohev Zedek Cemetery on Hamilton Mountain. Her casket, bought for $3,000, was ornate and similar to the one that had borne Rudolph Valentino to his final resting place.

Perri offered an open invitation to the public to come to the viewing on Sunday 17 August and by noon the crowds were so thick that traffic had come to a standstill. The number was later estimated at 25,000 spectators and, in the oppressive heat, fights began to break out.

The funeral began at 2:00 p.m. After it was over, the funeral cortège and hundreds of cars containing spectators set off for the cemetery. When they reached the gravesite, pandemonium reigned. Rocco Perri fainted, almost falling into the grave.

The letters spelling out "Perri" were later pried off the tombstone, which now reads simply *"TOBEN/STARKMAN/I.L.M.O./Bessie Starkman/ June 21 1890–Aug. 13, 1930."*

Margaret Houghton

THOMAS HENRY PRATT
(1850-1936)
Buried in Hamilton Cemetery, 777 York Boulevard,
Section Church of the Ascension — C

Thomas Pratt had a long, prominent and profitable business career. His first partner was Frederick Watkins, of the Right House fame, and they built up a general dry-goods business into the modern department store. In 1899, Pratt sold off his partnership and began his independent business, the T.H. Pratt Co. His advertisement in the *Spectator* declared, "We will fire the first shot on Thursday morning at 9 o'clock. We are out for game and our gun is loaded. We are ready for the fight and in good shape."

Pratt was also a director of the Hamilton, Grimsby and Beamsville Electric Railway, director of the Hamilton Stock-Yards Co., Ltd., chaired the Municipal Building Committee and sat on the Board of Health.

Pratt's primary interest for more than 30 years was the Hamilton General Hospital. He was an original member of the board of directors, established in 1896. He was the dominant force that transformed the institution into a modern centre. He sought to develop and maintain a high

The Hamilton General Hospital on Barton Street East in 1899.

level of health care. He was instrumental in having hospital regulations tightened, and pressed hard for expansion of the hospital to meet the growing needs for services and better facilities for the care and treatment of patients. His influence resulted in increased funding and the building of two new wings.

Pratt was also a trustee of the Boy's Home and the Hamilton Day Nursery, a director of the Aged Women's Home, vice-president of the Children's Aid Society, a member of the Society for the Prevention of Cruelty to Animals and a mason of Barton Lodge.

Mayor Thomas William Jutten once remarked that he had "never seen his equal for work on independent boards."

When Thomas Pratt died in 1936, his estate was valued at over $63,000.

Donna Reid & Robin McKee

ANDREW PRINDEL
(1780-1855)
Buried in Bowman United Church Cemetery, Highway #53, Ancaster

Andrew Prindel was a minister of the Methodist Episcopal Church, and was the first probationer of Canadian birth to serve that denomination. He was likely the son of William Prindel of Fredericksburgh, a United Empire Loyalist, and received an Order in Council for a land grant in 1808.

He started preaching in 1806 on the Ottawa Circuit, served the next year on the Yonge Street Circuit, and in 1808 at Litchfield, New York. In 1809, he was sent to the Ancaster Circuit, where he served a term. A subsequent posting was Washington Church, Scarborough (1811). The next mention of him is in 1828, when he retired from the active ministry and made his home in the Ancaster area. He continued to serve as a supply minister, and was part of the Dumfries Circuit in 1830. Information about his family is scanty and, while his wife is buried at Bowman, her name is not recorded. A daughter, Nancy (1817–1878), married Enoch Smith, perhaps the son of Jacob Smith of Glanford.

A notebook survives, kept by Prindel, which shows that he was paid in goods, noting 13 pounds of mutton and seven candles. The church at Bowman in the 1820s was noted as being of log, with galleries, and capable of seating 400.

Prindel's claim to interest is his size. He retired because of an ailment that caused his body to become very large, and it is reported that he weighed over 400 pounds. He had to have a special buggy constructed, with heavily reinforced springs. As well, there is a chair at Bowman Church specially constructed for him, significantly larger than an ordinary chair.

Paul Grimwood

RICHARD QUANCE
(1821-1900)
Buried in Christ Church Cemetery, Woodburn

Richard Quance was mentioned in the 1875 Wentworth County Atlas as one of the prominent men of Wentworth County. Richard christened on 16 July 1821 in Thornbury, Devon, England, the son of John and Mary Quance, formerly of Shebbear, Devon, England.

In 1843, Richard, his parents and his siblings decided to leave Devon and immigrated to Canada. It was a very stormy passage of six weeks. The ship was a hundred miles closer to England at the end of the second week than it was after one week. After arriving in Canada, they looked for the best property to settle, and the family finally settled in Binbrook, Wentworth County.

Richard had become acquainted with Alice Dayman, from Cornwall, on the ship from England. Her widower father and two brothers accompanied Alice on the trip. The Dayman family settled in Flamborough. In 1846, Richard and Alice were married in Flamborough and settled in Binbrook Township. They had a daughter and seven sons, several of whom later went to Delhi and built Quance's sawmill and grist mill.

Richard Quance built a shanty on his newly acquired land, located at Concession 1, Block 3, Lots 4 and 5 in the midst of the woods. In 1849, a much-needed sawmill was erected on the acquired land. The sawmill proved to be of great benefit to the farmers, supplying them with lumber for buildings to be built locally. Prior to this sawmill being built, the lumber had to be brought in from far distances.

In 1857, the sawmill burned down and Richard promptly rebuilt it. The sawmill and lumber business employed a large number of men. A large brick home was built to replace the shanty, also large barns and outbuildings. Richard Quance, by hard work, honesty and perseverance, succeeded to become a pillar of the community. Richard Quance served as reeve of Binbrook in 1883 and 1884.

The atlas states:

> He takes an active interest in all, which pertains to the welfare and elevation of those around him, and is respected and looked up to as an honest and honourable man in every way. Success has crowned Mr. Quance's efforts, success which is well merited.

Richard Quance died on 10 January 1900 at his son's home in Oakville, aged 78 years. He is buried in Christ Church Cemetery, Woodburn.

Shirley (Quance) Rumbles

ELIZABETH "BESSIE" RIDLER
(1817-1903)
Buried in Grove Cemetery, Dundas, North Quarter

When beloved teacher Bessie Ridler died on 21 April 1903 at the age of 86, more than 100 of her former pupils attended her funeral. Between 1849 and 1902, she taught scores of young Wilsons, McKenzies, Graftons, Bertrams and many others from the ages of five to twelve. For more than 50 years, her private school nurtured the growing young minds of the town's leading families, people who would grow and shape the destiny of the town of Dundas for generations.

The classroom itself was a large front room of her residence at 34 Hatt Street in Dundas (now the address of the Ellen Osler Memorial Home). It had two entrances — one for the boys, one for the girls. In the centre of the room was a large table; boys sat on one side, girls on the other, with Miss

Ridler, the ruling queen of the domain, at the head. Beside her on the table sat a basket, which housed the sometimes-dreaded ivory-tipped pencil, used for marking the lessons of the day.

The typical school day started off with arithmetic and writing, followed by spelling, geography, history and home economics, including sewing. The boys as well as the girls mastered the fine art of the needle and thread. It was not uncommon to walk by the school and hear the furious scrawling of chalk on slate and angelic choruses of "Yes, Miss Ridler" and "No, Miss Ridler." As children grew older, school books were handed down from elder to younger siblings.

Bessie Ridler lived with her brother George in the house on Hatt Street where she strived "to create a heroic pride in well doing" in her young subjects. She was a little woman whose good-humoured face was incapable of a

Miss Ridler's School on Hatt Street.

frown, and her pleasant disposition allowed her to be loved by all her students — and they did not soon forget what she taught them. Bessie Ridler never married or had children of her own.

She is buried in Grove Cemetery. Her epitaph reads: "The last enemy that shall be destroyed is death." Perhaps the love she lavished on and lessons she passed on to her students allowed her to do just that.

Stan Nowak

GEORGE ROLPH
(1794–1875)
Buried in Grove Cemetery, Dundas, North Quarter

It happened around midnight; he had opened the door of his Dundas residence to see a gang of masked men. The men seized him, dragged him out, beat him senseless, and literally tarred and feathered him. Despite his many good deeds before and after that infamous night, George Rolph is chiefly remembered for the "tar and feather outrage" that occurred on the evening of 3 June 1826.

Mr Rolph was a wealthy businessman and landowner who had arrived in Dundas in 1816 from Gloucester, England. He was the Clerk of the Peace, clerk of the District Court and registrar of the Surrogate Court, and also practised law in Dundas and Ancaster for more than 50 years. He was a very private man who did not socialize well with his fellow citizens, but he was generous to them. He owned one-quarter of Dundas, but allowed the flat, open part of his property to be used as a village common. Everyone in town was welcome to use what is now the Dundas Driving Park. At his own expense he built Sydenham Road, completed in 1843. He donated stone from his quarry to build St Augustine's Church. So why was he subjected to the "outrage"?

Some claim it was his politics. He was a Reformer, but tried to hide the fact from the powerful Tories of the day, such as Allan MacNab and Dr James Hamilton.

There was his personal life. Being almost a recluse, he kept his 300-acre estate heavily fenced with two iron gates at the entrances, one of which was later used for Dundurn Castle; it is on the York Street entrance today.

The defence of the accused was that they acted on moral grounds. Within that heavily fenced estate, the very married Mr Rolph was allegedly having an affair with his housekeeper.

The accused included nine prominent Tories of the day, including Allan MacNab. At the trial, only two of them were found guilty and fined.

The Rolph Gates, now at Dundurn Castle

Rolph continued to live in Dundas and enjoyed a successful legal career, but was never really accepted by his fellow townfolk. He died on 25 July 1875 at the age of 81, and is buried in Grove Cemetery along with his mother, wife and son.

Stan Nowak

SARAH OLIVE ROUTLEDGE
(1885-1922)
Buried in Hamilton Cemetery, 777 York Boulevard, Section Y

Local history buffs know that Rocco Perri and his partner-wife Bessie Starkman were Hamilton's most notorious crime couple. Bessie, the business brain of the racketeering and bootlegging duo, was gunned down outside their Bay Street South home in 1930. Rocco went to buy cigarettes in 1944 and was never seen again.

Sarah Olive Routledge played a pivotal, but lesser known, role in the lives of Perri and Starkman.

Sarah Routledge moved from Bancroft to Hamilton in 1917 and began work in a knitting mill. Soon, she began to "keep company" with Rocco

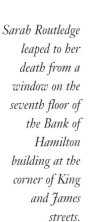

Sarah Routledge leaped to her death from a window on the seventh floor of the Bank of Hamilton building at the corner of King and James streets.

Perri, who did not reveal to her his real name or the fact he was involved with Bessie Starkman.

Routledge became pregnant and gave birth to a daughter named Autumn. Perri refused to marry Routledge, but agreed to provide child support. Routledge, who had told her family and friends she was married, fled to St Catharines.

In 1920, Sarah Routledge resumed her affair with Rocco Perri and gave birth to a second daughter. On 11 February 1922 she visited her lawyer in connection with Perri's support agreement. A few days later Routledge left her older child at the hospital with apparent food poisoning. At 1:00 a.m. the next morning she took her youngest child to a late-night diner and asked two men to watch the child while she made a phone call. Then she disappeared.

Police rounded up Routledge and her children. Under interrogation she admitted her involvement with Rocco Perri.

Shortly thereafter, Routledge met with Perri's lawyer. During the course of the conversation, Routledge was incorrectly told Perri was already married to Bessie Starkman. Apparently, Routledge had not known the whole truth about Starkman. It is not clear how much Starkman knew about Sarah Routledge.

After being left alone for a brief time in her lawyer's office, Routledge climbed out the seventh-storey window and plummeted to her death on the King Street pavement.

An inquest was held. No charges were levelled against Rocco Perri.

Sarah Routledge's two children were released to the custody of her parents.

Ronald Berenbaum

ROYAL AIR FORCE SERVICEMEN
(1941–1943)
Buried at St Paul's Glanford Anglican Church, Mount Hope

Thirteen Anson twin-engined aircraft flew out of No. 33 R.A.F. Navigation Training School at Mount Hope on the night of 13 November 1941, on navigational exercises. Twelve returned. In the deteriorating weather that night, the crew of Anson W1672, while trying to get below cloud cover, crashed their plane in the Caledon Hills. Killed were Leading Aircraftsmen Dennis Donahue, Denis Drayton and Reginald Gillman. They were buried in St Paul's Church cemetery less than a mile from the runway from which they had flown on that training flight. They were the first of 14 airmen stationed at Mount Hope who died over a period of 25 months. All 14 of these servicemen were buried at St Paul's.

The crash of Anson aircraft 6767 on 23 June 1942, took the heaviest loss of life. Eyewitnesses watched as this plane, flying in a westerly direction, suddenly turned over out of control, went into a dive and crashed at Bedford Farm, Wallacetown, southwest of London. Killed were Leading Aircraftman James Watson, Sergeant Herbert Preston, Corporal Colin Campbell, Sergeant Pilot Edward Doughty and Flight Lieutenant John Kellow. Kellow had participated in the first bombing raid on enemy-occupied France 18 days previously.

Twelve days before Christmas, 1942, Anson R6709 was being flown on a night navigational assignment. Sergeant Richard Board and Leading Aircraftsmen Charles Chadwick and Ernest Johnson were killed when this aircraft crashed near Avon, Ontario.

Flying Officer Peter Scott A.F.C., who died of natural causes 1 May 1943, in the station hospital of No. 16 Flying Training School at Hagersville, and Aircraftman Stephen Proudly, who lost his life in a motor car accident in Hamilton on June 10 that same year, were the only airmen buried here who didn't die in plane crashes.

Leading Aircraftman Taunton Pouyat was flying in Anson 6930, which collided in mid-air with another aircraft and crashed at Waterford. He died 7 December 1943 from the resulting injuries.

To train or be trained as navigators for the rapidly expanding Royal Air Force, these 14, all from Great Britain, had left their beleaguered islands never to return. The names of these aviators are commemorated in the Royal Air Force Book of Remembrance in St Clement Danes Church in the Strand in London, England.

But locally, too, these men are remembered. After World War II, for more than 50 years, the Junior Farmers of Wentworth County have honoured these 14 servicemen at a special decoration service. In the fall of 2000, a Remembrance Garden was dedicated to the memory of the RAF members buried at St Paul's.

Reginald Gillman, Dennis Donahue, Denis Drayton, John Kellow, Herbert Preston, Edward Doughty, James Watson, Colin Campbell, Charles Chadwick, Ernest Johnson, Richard Board, Peter Scott, Stephen Proudly, Taunton Pouyat

At the going down of the sun and in the morning we shall remember them.

Art French

SAMUEL RYCKMAN
(1777-1846)
Buried in the Ryckman Family Cemetery, Ryckman's Corners

At least four generations of the Ryckman pioneer family are buried in a little fenced cemetery on a knoll in a field of the old family farm.

Samuel Ryckman immigrated to Canada sometime after the American Revolution and acted as a Crown land surveyor. For payment, he was granted 700 acres, which included all four corners of what are now Upper James Street (Highway #6) and Rymal Road (Highway #53). The area is known as Ryckman's Corners, named after Samuel.

Samuel built a log house and barn, cleared about 26 acres of land and took up farming full-time.

One of the most unusual stones in the cemetery is a low round-topped one that reads, "Old Uncle Joe, Died Dec. 26, 1868, Aged 69 Years." "Joe" was possibly a black man, who may have escaped slavery from the United States before the Civil War. The Ryckmans would have taken him in as a hired hand and, as a simple gesture for his faithful service, allowed him to have his last resting place in the family cemetery.

Ironically, although Samuel was the Crown surveyor, the intersection of Highway #6 and Highway #53 has always been badly offset. This jog in the road has been reduced over the years, but it is still there today. The jog did not seem to bother the early pioneers, who established their farms and businesses at the Corners. The curve in the road attests to Samuel's misreading the needs of future generations.

Donna Reid & Robin McKee

MAE BELLE SAMPSON
(1890-1918)

A memorial plaque to Mae Belle Sampson was unveiled at the
Hamilton General Hospital on 14 December 1920

Mae Belle Sampson was born at Duntroon, near Collingwood, and began her training in 1910 at Hamilton General Hospital. Three years later she graduated with the McLaren scholarship and a gold medal. She worked as a private nurse for a year and then enlisted for overseas service in World War I, the first local nurse to do so.

In September 1914 she went to France as a member of the Canadian Army Medical Corps. She served in a stationary Canadian hospital for two years and then worked at the Canadian Casualty Clearing Station in Flanders from 1915 to 1916. Then she transferred to the Salonika front where she was stationed for a year.

In March 1918 she was assigned as nurse on the *SS Llandovery Castle*, a hospital ship that travelled between England and Canada, bringing back

Mae Bell Sampson (centre) graduating from the Hamilton General Hospital School of Nursing.

Canadian wounded. On 27 June 1918 the ship, although marked as a hospital ship with a large red cross, was torpedoed and sunk by a German submarine. As it broke off, the stern of the ship swamped the lifeboat bearing the 14 nursing sisters. They all perished. The Germans attacked the remaining lifeboats as well and only one boat survived.

Mae Belle Sampson's death was confirmed on 5 July 1918. She was remembered in Hamilton by a plaque in the Hamilton General Hospital's entrance hall: "To the glory of God and in honoured memory of Nursing Sister Mae Belle Sampson, C.A.M.C., who made the supreme sacrifice in the sinking of the S.S. Llandovery Castle, June 17, 1918. Her soul liveth!"

Her name was also included in the hospital's roll of honour, designed and presented by William Bruce the same day as the installation of the plaque.

In 1939 she was honoured by the First Contingent Club, which placed a plaque behind the president's chair "to be one more reminder of the sacrifices that a passing generation once made."

Margaret Houghton

HARRIET (VAUX) SANFORD
(1849-1938)
*Buried in Hamilton Cemetery, 777 York Boulevard,
Section Christ's Church Cathedral — E*

Harriet (Vaux) Sanford, at the age of 17 in 1866, became the second wife of Senator William Eli Sanford. For six years prior to Eli's appointment to the senate in 1887, Harriet and Eli Sanford travelled the world collecting art and other valuable furnishings for their stately home in Hamilton. It became one of the most spectacular private residences of its time. The home was on the block bounded by Jackson Street, Bay Street, Hunter Street and Caroline Street, and the house faced Caroline. Architect William Stewart did the 1892 remodelling. The house exterior was brown and grey sandstone. There were 56 rooms including 5 bathrooms and, at this time, the house had an assessed value of $35,000. It was one of the first houses in Hamilton expressly wired for electricity. It was at this time that the house was named Wesanford after the owner. William Eli Sanford drowned at his summer residence at Lake Rosseau in 1899, and his widow lived in the house until her death in 1938.

Harriet Sanford was involved in the National Council of Women from its formation in 1893 and served for many years as president. She was also involved with the formation of the Victorian Order of Nurses, served as a member of the International Council of Women (the only Canadian woman

Harriet (Vaux)
Sanford in
1903.

among its officers) and was president of such varied groups as the Women's
Association and Women's Missionary Society, the Home for the Friendless
and Infant's Home and the Ladies' Auxiliary of the Wentworth Historical
Society. She belonged to such other groups as the Social Service Council of
Canada, the Women's Canadian Club, the Hamilton Health Association and
the Imperial Order Daughters of the Empire. She and her daughters took an

active interest in Elsinore, the convalescent home for working girls, which had been founded on the Beach by her husband. She died, in her 90th year, in 1938.

Margaret Houghton

WILLIAM ELI SANFORD
(1838-1899)
Buried in Hamilton Cemetery, 777 York Blvd,
Section Christ's Church Cathedral — E

An orphan from Connecticut grew up to be the Wool King of Canada.

The W.E. Sanford Manufacturing Company on King Street East.

After the death of both parents, William Sanford moved to Hamilton and was raised by his uncle, Edward Jackson. He initially partnered in a successful foundry in London, Ontario, but when his wife died he returned to Hamilton.

The American Civil War created a demand for woollen fabric and Sanford quickly responded with exported goods. But Sanford was a visionary. At the time, woollen fabric went to tailors to be made into clothing,

The Sanford, McInnes & Co. clothing store on King Street East in 1860.

including military uniforms. The process, with fittings and single-unit production, was lengthy and expensive for the customer.

In partnership with Alexander MacInnes, Sanford built a factory to produce reasonably priced good-quality ready-made clothing. For the first time a man could enter a store, request his size and exit with a pair of trousers that fit. The concept was an immediate success.

With newly designed cutting machines, losses were minimal and productivity increased rapidly. At their peak, the factories produced 800 pairs of pants and 350 suits per day. There were contracts for military uniforms for both the British and Canadian governments. A wholesale operation was set up in Winnipeg to develop business in western Canada. Showrooms were opened in Toronto, Montreal, Ottawa, Calgary and Vancouver.

In 1872, Sanford created the Oak Hall Stores to retail the goods he manufactured. In addition to clothes for men and children, the stores sold ready-made boots and shoes. In 1884, W. E. Sanford and Company was one of Hamilton's largest manufacturers, with more than 2,000 employees.

Sanford and his second wife, Harriet Sophia (Vaux), were benefactors to many charities and educational organizations, including the Wesleyan Ladies' College and the Royal Canadian Humane Association. Elsinore, on the Beach strip, was opened as a summer haven for underprivileged children to escape the heat and pollution of the city.

In 1887, in recognition of his contributions to Canadian society and his support of Sir John A. Macdonald, Sanford was made a senator.

William Eli Sanford remained active in the company he created until his death. He drowned while at his cottage on Lake Rosseau in 1899. In 1922, the assets of the W. E. Sanford Manufacturing Company were liquidated and the equipment sold at auction. In 1930, the head office building was demolished to make way for an addition to the Royal Connaught Hotel.

Donna Reid & Robin McKee

WILLIAM OSCAR SEALEY
(1859-1940)
Buried in Hamilton Cemetery, 777 York Boulevard,
Section Church of the Ascension — C

His formal education consisted of attending Waterdown Public and Grammar School only until the age of 12, but W.O. Sealey is regarded as one of Waterdown's famous sons from his successful career in later life, when he was elected to Wentworth County Council and, from 1908, as a member of the Dominion Parliament.

After leaving school, he worked at a variety of jobs, including operating a large general store at Main and Dundas Streets. It was while there, living above the store, that he was involved in one of the most dramatic incidents in Waterdown's history.

Within the store, Sealey also carried on a banking business. During the early hours of 14 April 1887, burglars searching for the downstairs safe broke into the building. The intruders drilled holes near the safe handle, inserted powder and ignited a fuse. The enormous explosion blew open the safe, shattered windows and awakened Sealey, who was in bed above.

Grabbing his revolver, he blasted away from the top of the stairway, hoping to scare the burglars, but they returned the fire and four bullets pierced the bedroom floor. Several more volleys of gunfire occurred before W.O. attempted to open a window and call for help. Finding them all stuck, he finally kicked out the glass in one window and began shouting. All the noise brought the burglars out onto the street where they retaliated with a hail of bullets.

The gunfire missed Sealey, who continued to shoot at the street below. Realizing that the noise would attract attention, the burglars began to beat a retreat, two running northwards and two across the Dundas Street intersection. The northbound pair carried the drawers from the safe, full of valuable papers, eventually throwing them under the Dundas Street bridge where they were found later that day.

Throughout the morning, villagers visited Sealey's general store to see the bullet holes and hear the details of the "bloodless battle," William Oscar assuring those who questioned him "that no money had been stolen, as he did not keep it in the safe, having learnt his lesson from an earlier robbery."

During his parliamentary years, Sealey and his wife lived in Hamilton. But in 1939, in failing health, he moved to the home of his nephew on South Street, Dundas, where he died 7 January 1940.

Sylvia Wray

TITUS GEER SIMONS
(1765-1829)
Buried in the Municipal Cemetery, Highway #8, Bullock's Corners, West Flamborough Township

One of the prominent early inhabitants at the Head-of-the-Lake, Titus Geer Simons was often controversial in his actions, and rarely apologetic. Born into a Connecticut family with Puritan ancestry, he marched with his father's

Titus Geer Simons

regiment during the American Revolutionary War, even though he was just 12 years old. The family fled northwards to Montreal after Burgoyne's defeat at Saratoga in 1777. At the end of hostilities, they moved to Upper Canada, where both father and son petitioned for land, settling eventually at Niagara.

Titus Geer Simons was appointed publisher of Upper Canada's only newspaper, *The Upper Canada Gazette or American Oracle*, on 20 September 1797 and immediately made promises "to print more news and provide a better service." The printing of the paper was transferred to York (Toronto) in 1800 under the name of Waters & Simons, King's Printers. Simons explained "his name was second only because of his younger age, and that he did most of the work." Waters and Simons were dismissed a year later after printing a controversial article, and for the editorial content of the paper.

Simons' political beliefs probably influenced his participation in the famous Tar and Feathers Case that took place in Dundas after a dinner party on the evening of 2 July 1826 at the home of Dr James Hamilton of West Flamborough. Besides Simons, other notable Tories at the supper included Allan MacNab and Alexander Robertson, all of whom decided to humiliate ardent Dundas Reformer, George Rolph, who had in their view outraged public morality by "living in an adulterous relationship."

The group blackened their faces and went to Rolph's home, expecting to find him "in the arms of a Mrs Evans" when they burst into his bedroom, but were disappointed, as he was alone. They grabbed Rolph, gagged, blindfolded and stripped him, smearing his body with tar and feathers from his own pillows and threatening him with bodily harm.

At the Gore Assizes the following year, Simons, Hamilton and Robertson stood accused of the crime, with the Solicitor General of Upper Canada acting for the defendants, assisted by lawyers Allan MacNab and Alexander Chewett, who had both taken part in the incident. Simons and Hamilton were each fined £20, rather than the £1,000 for which they were sued. Undaunted, the two solicited contributions from the residents of West Flamborough to pay their fines.

Sylvia Wray

ERNEST D'ISRAELI SMITH
(1853-1948)
Buried at Stoney Creek Cemetery

E.D. Smith came from a proud Loyalist background, but during his own lifetime brought his family name to national prominence and carved out a personal fiefdom centred on Winona. By the time of his death his company,

E.D. Smith & Sons, controlled vast stretches of territory, dominated the local economy and exerted considerable political and social power in the community.

His unusual name was derived from the affection of his mother, Damaris, for the British Prime Minister Benjamin Disraeli. First educated at Winona Public School, E.D. trained to be an engineer like his brother, Cecil, but poor eyesight forced E.D. into an ultimately much more successful career as an agricultural entrepreneur.

"One has to be sharp in business and not rely on men's honour for any-thing," he wrote in his autobiography after losing business to his cousin, Ransom. Ransom filled E.D.'s customers' peach orders with his own produce while E.D. was away on business in 1880.

E.D.'s masterstroke was to specialize his farming operations increasingly towards fruit production and eventually its derivations like jam, ketchup and sauces. He also was very successful in the floral nurseries business and in landscaping.

E.D. Smith combined his shrewd business acumen with a fierce intellect and political ambitions. Although unsuccessful in running for Township Council in 1878–9, he succeeded in 1880 and began a six-decade career in government. A Conservative MP in Ottawa from 1900 to 1910, he was appointed to the Senate in 1913 by Robert Borden. Even at the end of his days, E.D. made political history, being the first Canadian senator not to die

E.D. Smith & Sons Ltd., Winona, in 1937.

in office. He resigned his post in 1946 for health reasons.

Ironically, the Fruit King himself had little appetite for rich food, due to a lifelong stomach disorder and a constant hectic schedule.

From his first days as councillor to his last years as senator, E.D. Smith and his descendants ran Winona. By 1939, the company not only had its own police and fire forces, but also built its own water system and provided subsidized housing to its workers and their families. The company sponsored its own militia regiment. By 1925, E.D. Smith's factory and farm complex was a community unto itself.

A fierce trade protectionist, E.D. pioneered the first Canadian jam factory (1905) and the first refrigerated railway cars (1900). He was surprisingly liberal in his social attitudes, assisting his wife Christina with the 1897 formation of the Women's Institutes movement. He chaired many community clubs (like the local Grange chapter), and donated money, land, produce and time to a variety of causes.

Michael Gemmell

TROY
(1989-1992)
Buried at the Ancaster Pet Cemetery, 330 Book Road East, Ancaster

"Police dogs are used with success elsewhere, let's give them a trial period here," recommended Police Chief Leonard G. Lawrence to the Board of Police Commissioners. The Board agreed. Since July 1, 1960, the citizens of Hamilton have benefited from this important decision to add the unique abilities of canines to the police service.

Formal training classes continue twice weekly, with additional daily drills keeping the dogs alert and in top physical condition. After the basic obedience training was over, they quickly learned how to find and fetch various articles like keys, bottles, wallets, tools and guns. Their keen noses enabled them to out-class their two legged colleagues in searching for lost persons, burglars hidden in large buildings or trailed through city streets and back alleys.

A word or gesture usually directs the dogs, but they will immediately defend their masters from attack, tackling even an armed person firing a gun at them.

In sharp contrast to this fierce courage in combat, both dogs are gentle enough to enjoy playful rough-and-tumble with the officers' young children.

Although they should not be considered as wonder dogs, they have already proven through their willing service to be an asset to the Hamilton Police Department.

Whenever a situation arises when the use of police dogs for searching or tracking seems likely, remember, it is extremely important not to foul the scent or track. Stand back and preserve the scene. Your co-operations and the handler's skill are both needed to gain the full benefits of our capable k-9s.

Hamilton Police Department Annual Report, 1960

Police dog Troy was killed in the line of duty, 26 February 1992, saving a police officer's life. He had been with the force for one year and was a two-and-a-half-year-old German Shepherd. He was the first member of the Police Canine Unit to be killed in the performance of his duty. Troy distracted a gunman who was pointing a rifle at another police officer, and was shot by the assailant and killed instantly.

Margaret Houghton

JAMES WILLIAMS TYRRELL, C.E., O.L.S., D.L.S.
(1863-1945)
Buried in Hamilton Cemetery, 777 York Boulevard, Section Y

The Tyrrell surname is synonymous with exploration in Canada. Raised in a large Irish family in Weston, Ontario, two Tyrrell brothers went on to explore and document much of Canada's frontier.

In 1884, while employed by the Geological Survey of Canada, Joseph Burr Tyrrell discovered the first dinosaur remains in Red Deer, Alberta.

That discovery, *Albertosaurus*, is on display in the Tyrrell Museum of Paleontology. He went on to survey much of northern Alberta, Manitoba and the Arctic.

Younger brother James Williams was more interested in outdoor sports than academics, but in his lifetime he would work as an interpreter, surveyor, engineer, prospector, cartographer and author. At 20 years old, he too began his career with the Geological Survey. His first assignment, in the Lake of the Woods region, resulted in a three-year commitment to exploring and mapping the area and in a fondness for the wilderness.

In 1888, after receiving his commissions as an Ontario Provincial and Dominion Land Surveyor, Tyrrell, with partner G.B. Abrey, opened a municipal engineering firm in Hamilton at 42 James Street North. Increased development in the region created a demand for surveys and accurate maps. Much of the area in Wentworth County and surrounding areas had not been surveyed since the 1790s. As a consequence, property lines were not clearly defined. In 1901, Tyrrell and his partners published the atlas of Wentworth County.

The lure of the north country was strong and Tyrrell took every opportunity to escape the city and visit the hinterlands. In 1893 he joined his

James Tyrrell on a surveying expedition.

The Tyrrell surveying party.

brother, Joseph, for an arduous eight-month journey from Lake Athabaska to Hudson Bay. He documented his experiences in *Across the Sub-Arctic of Canada* published in 1897.

James Tyrrell surveyed mining claims in the Klondike and, from 1903 until 1910, he surveyed many townships in Alberta, Saskatchewan and Manitoba. When he was refused active duty in World War I, he returned to Hamilton to resume his engineering practice. He kept an active role in surveying northern mining sites, but also found time to enjoy his farm, the Beverly Ranch.

Tyrrell served as an alderman, then city controller from 1914 to 1918. He never lost his love of the north country and, in his late 70s, he was known to still portage his canoe in the wilderness.

Donna Reid & Robin McKee

RICHARD MOTT WANZER
(1818-1900)
Buried in Hamilton Cemetery, 777 York Boulevard, Section E9-11

Richard Mott Wanzer was born in New York State of Quaker parents. After years in various business ventures in the States, by the late 1850s he found himself in financial difficulties. His solution to his problem was to move to Hamilton.

Upon his arrival in 1859, Wanzer and his nephew set up a sewing-machine factory at the corner of James and Vine Streets. The reasoning behind his move to Hamilton had been to avoid the restrictions on American manufacturing patents. Since United States patent protection did not extend to Canada at this time, Wanzer could incorporate patented ideas into his Canadian sewing-machine manufacturing without paying royalties to the American patent holders. Very shortly after starting manufacturing, his door-to-door salesmen could not keep up with the demand for the four models of machine he offered.

The demand led Wanzer to entering into partnership with John Tarbox to finance the move to a bigger factory. The new facility at the corner of King and Catharine Streets employed 400 men, attracting many skilled mechanics. Wanzer bought out Tarbox in 1875 for $100,000 and began to expand the factory again, building a new facility on Barton Street. Wanzer now employed 800 workers who produced 2,000 machines per week.

In the 1880s, competition from American manufacturers, as well as economic uncertainty, was having an impact on his business. He diversified, getting into the manufacture of coal oil lamps, but nothing was enough to save the company. In 1892 he went into bankruptcy and his creditors seized all his assets. W.E. Sanford, a friend of Wanzer's, purchased from the credi-

The Wanzer Sewing Machine Factory on King Street East at Catherine Street.

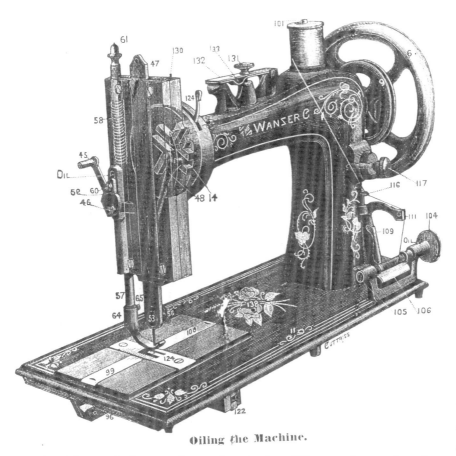

Oiling the Machine.

The Wanzer Sewing Machine.

tors the rights to the lamp and gave them back to Wanzer, who continued to manufacture and promote their manufacture.

When he died while on business in New York in 1900, his body was returned to Hamilton, his adopted home, and lay in state in the council chamber of Hamilton's City Hall while the city flag was flown at half-staff.

Margaret Houghton

THOMAS C. WATKINS
(1818-1903)
Buried in Hamilton Cemetery, 777 York Boulevard, Section A8

Thomas Watkins was a retired teacher who became a retailer when he opened his first store in Hamilton in 1847. In 1875, he began construction of a new modern building at the corner of King and Hughson Streets. The Right House was designed by the Hamilton architectural firm of William Stewart and Company, and was completed in 1893. When the building

An early delivery wagon for Thomas Watkins' Right House.

opened, it was considered to be among the finest and most expensive stores in the city, carrying a large selection of dry goods, carpets, household furnishings and fancy goods. It was known as the Crystal Palace due to the extensive use of plate glass, and was fireproofed using an early example of reinforced concrete. The six-floor building was Hamilton's first skyscraper of the 1890s. There were many other firsts incorporated into the building and the Watkins business: he installed telephones that connected different departments; he hired female clerks, advertised on a large scale, established a charge account system and developed a local delivery system.

Thomas Watkins was the driving force behind the family enterprise that lasted over 100 years.

The Right House was lovingly restored in the 1980s and is the last 19th century department store to survive in downtown Hamilton.

Donna Reid & Robin McKee

ISABELLA (HYDE) WHYTE
(1787-1865)
Buried in Hamilton Cemetery, 777 York Boulevard, Section Christ's Church Cathedral — A

The story of Isabella Hyde Whyte is one of Hamilton's most enduring legends. The Duke of Kent and his mistress Madame Julie de St Laurent lived together until he married to try to have a legitimate heir. In 1819 Princess

Alexandrina Victoria was born. Eight months later, Edward died and his daughter later became Queen Victoria.

No definitive proof has ever been found that any children were born to Edward and Julie, although one historian documents 12 children. Many local historians, however, have published as fact that Isabella was the first of these supposed children. Also published was the assertion that the royal family arranged a suitable marriage for Isabella with John Whyte. It was stated that the couple moved to Hamilton when Queen Victoria came to the throne in 1839 to avoid embarrassing the royal family.

A wonderful story and a great legend, but what is the truth?

Isabella Hyde was born in 1787 to Ruth and Charles Hyde. Charles Hyde was an apothecary and surgeon practising in London, England. On 29 August 1807, Isabella married Charles Boyd. Although at first everything went well, by 1808 the couple had begun quarrelling. In the early months of 1809 Isabella met John Whyte and a relationship quickly developed. They met often secretly throughout that summer. Charles Boyd became suspicious and followed them to an inn on 8 September. Charles barged in, demanding to see his wife, who attempted to escape down the stairs but was caught. The next day she packed her things and moved in with John Whyte. On 26 January 1810 Charles Boyd filed a suit for divorce. The case dragged on for two years until, in 1812, the Court of Arches granted a decree of separation and divorce to Charles. What this meant was that they were divorced, but that neither party could remarry while the other party still lived.

Barton Lodge, the home of the Whyte family on Hamilton mountain.

Between 1811 and 1827, John and Isabella had four children — one son and three daughters.

In 1847 John Whyte, Isabella Boyd and their surviving daughter, Emily, moved to Hamilton. They settled into Barton Lodge, a grand house on the edge of the escarpment built by John's brother, James, who had died in 1843. John Whyte died in 1862. Isabella died 11 February 1865. They are both buried in the Hamilton Cemetery. Their daughter Emily Gourlay lived in Hamilton until her death in 1905. The family remained at Barton Lodge until it was destroyed by fire in 1930.

Margaret Houghton

YOUNG CEMETERY

This cemetery is located on the east side of Upper Wellington Street, between Stone Church Road and Rymal Road (Highway #53)

Daniel Young (1755–1836), a loyalist settler, bought 100 acres at Ryckman's Corners in 1806. He became one of the earliest farmers on the Mountain. Daniel's earlier life was a far cry from his tranquil life as a farmer. During the American Revolution, Daniel and his brother John escaped to join the Loyalist forces on the Niagara frontier. They served for years with the famous Butler's Rangers, raiding America. After the hostilities, the Young family settled along the Grand River, and it was John who, by marrying a Mohawk woman, secured the property still known as the Young Tract. This was the first white settlement in Haldimand County.

When Daniel died in 1836, he left his land to his children. The earliest recorded burial here is from 1878, making the burial site of Daniel unknown. Even though the family eventually sold the farm, the sale always carried a provision excluding the burial plot.

What is reputed to be Hamilton's first murder mystery is connected with the Young family farm property. In 1827, Daniel Young's son John and his grandson Christopher were accused of murdering a farm employee, Jesse Masters, in the coal-pit, or kiln, situated on the property. No corpse was ever found, and so at the trial they were found not guilty. In 1830, to clear the family name, family members succeeded in finding Jesse Masters, alive and living in New York State, restoring the good family's reputation.

Daniel's eldest son, James, and his direct family members are the ones that are buried in the Young Cemetery.

Donna Reid & Robin McKee

An early view of the Burlington Bay Canal showing the first Royal Hamilton Yacht Club.

EDWARD ZEALAND
(ca 1793–1869)
Buried in Hamilton Cemetery, 777 York Boulevard, Section A6

Edward Zealand was born in Yorkshire, England, and was renowned for a long and illustrious naval career. At the age of 12 he joined the Royal Navy, and was said to have served under British Admiral Lord Nelson.

During the War of 1812, Zealand was a member of the British Naval Squadron patrolling the St Lawrence River and the Great Lakes, and may have served with Sir James Yeo during the Lake Ontario encounters of 1813.

After the war, Zealand settled in Hamilton and commanded a number of commercial lake schooners plying between Dundas, Hamilton and York (Toronto). One of his earliest commands was the *Rebecca*, which was the first lake vessel to deliver cargo to the new port of Hamilton following the opening of the Burlington Canal in 1826.

In 1834 Zealand commanded the steamship *Constitution*, thus making the transition from sail to steam.

During the Rebellion of 1837, Zealand accompanied Sir Allan MacNab on his raid on William Lyon Mackenzie's provisional headquarters on Navy

Island in the Niagara River. Zealand commanded one of the boarding vessels, which helped to transport about 60 men to the *Caroline*, the steamship used by the rebels to amass goods and ammunition. One man was killed during the raid, and the ship was torched and set adrift over Niagara Falls. This caused an international incident for, in fact, MacNab's men had invaded the United States during this raid. Fortunately for Canada, the United States government did not pursue or protest the transgression.

In 1840 Zealand established his own wharf and forwarding business, and by 1847 was operating three schooners. In 1861 Zealand formed the Naval Brigade of Hamilton to guard against a possible American invasion as a result of the outbreak of the Civil War.

Zealand was one of the earliest commodores of the Royal Hamilton Yacht Club and was instrumental in the placement of two Crimean War cannons in Harvey Park.

Edward Zealand was killed on MacNab Street when a cow, which had escaped from the market, gored him. He was buried with full military honours in the Hamilton Cemetery.

Donna Reid & Robin McKee

An illustration of the steamship Caroline.

EPILOGUE

Where there are people, there are cemeteries. It is a given, in any form of civilization, that the dead are memorialized. Informal family plots are set up on farms as soon as people settle and more formal cemeteries are created not long after. Early graves on farms were usually marked with simple wooden markers that have disappeared as the elements wore them away.

During the late 18th and early 19th centuries in Ontario, a particular type of gravestone style began to be seen. This style was comparable to the style of the New England states and upper New York State, which is logical considering the number of settlers who arrived from there after the Revolutionary War. The basic shape was a rectangular slab generally 3½ to 4 feet tall and 2 feet wide. In Ontario they were almost exclusively stone, and the stone most commonly used was white marble. Unfortunately, this type of stone weathers quickly and unevenly so that the surface is obliterated and the text lost. This type of stone was also very susceptible to fungus, which ate away the stone. Marble cutters in marble works locally carved most of the markers. The standard format was a design of some sort on the top of the monument followed by an epitaph.

The epitaphs were generally standard verses, quite often from the Bible, that were common across the province. Reading the text on early tombstones can be rather depressing, with references to "flesh mouldering in the tomb," "call'd hence by early doom," or "Our life, how short — a groan, a sigh;/We live and then begin to die." Marx Binkley's tombstone in the old Binkley Cemetery in West Hamilton reads

> *When I am dead and buried*
> *And all my bones are rotten*
> *When this you see, oh think of me*
> *Lest I should be forgotten*

The Binkley Cemetery is one of literally dozens of small cemeteries around Hamilton. Some are family plots on property once owned by early settlers and others are small church cemeteries. St Peter's Cemetery on Mohawk Road started as the Rymal family cemetery and then St Peter's Anglican Church, Barton, opened beside it on 23 June 1853. This church was closed in 1884 and subsequently torn down but the cemetery still takes its name from the church. The tombstones record such early names as Almas, Ryckman, Terryberry, Secord and Rousseaux. Near this old cemetery is the Hess Family Burial Ground at St Bartholomew's Anglican Church, Mohawk Road near Garth Street.

There are three major cemeteries in the Hamilton area: the Hamilton Cemetery, Holy Sepulchre Cemetery and Woodland Cemetery.

The Hamilton Cemetery is on the raised stretch of land at the west end of the bay, commonly known as Burlington Heights. A military stronghold during the War of 1812, the first section of this land to be used for cemetery purposes was purchased from Sir Allan MacNab in 1847 by Christ's Church Cathedral. The city acquired part of this tract in 1848 and called it Burlington Cemetery. Other sections of land were purchased as they became available. In 1857 the ground's old gates were replaced, and some time after 1865 the Cemetery Lodge and Chapel were built. In 1892 the two separate church burying grounds (Christ's Church Cathedral and Church of the Ascension) entered into an agreement with City Council to hand over these properties to the city for general care. With this agreement, the name of the cemetery was changed to Hamilton Cemetery. The Hamilton Cemetery was the first municipally owned and operated cemetery in Canada. The Cemetery Board began operating in June of 1899, replacing an earlier rather haphazard system, and set about fixing up the cemetery with proper roadways, improved water and drainage systems, level grades and a general improvement in the appearance of the cemetery.

They needed to find a way to finance this work so they introduced a system of annual care by which plot owners were charged an annual fee. This was not a success as some refused to pay, many were indifferent and many relatives had moved away and could not be found. In 1916 the system of perpetual care was established. A percentage of the price of the lot was set aside to provide for future care. Perpetual care is now mandated for all cemeteries across Ontario.

There was a long list of rules and regulations regarding conduct in the cemetery, which included prohibitions against horses travelling faster than a walk, children under the age of 12 unless accompanied by an adult, bicycles being driven over graves, picnickers, smoking, picking flowers, dogs, discharging firearms, removing rocks, writing on anything and improper conduct. The gates were locked overnight and no entrance was allowed after 9:00 p.m.

By 1926 all the plots in the separate church sections had been sold so the churches relinquished control of their sections to the city.

The Catholic Church in Hamilton has always maintained a separate cemetery, as canonical or church law required Roman Catholics to be buried in a grave blessed or consecrated by the church. An early church cemetery on the site of what is now the Cathedral of Christ the King fell into disrepair and the decision was made to find another plot of land. In August of 1874 land was purchased on the north shore of the harbour. The Bishop of

Hamilton, the Right Reverend Peter Francis Crinnon, formally blessed this land on 15 November 1875. Holy Sepulchre, as this cemetery became known, continued to acquire land. On 20 April 1889, Bishop Dowling laid the cornerstone of the mortuary chapel. The *Hamilton Spectator* described the plan of the chapel as "a cut stone structure of Gothic style, with buttresses, chancel and belfry. The dimensions are 25 x 40 feet with an apse 8 x 12 feet. A basement of the same dimension, and 8 feet in height is provided as a vault for the reception of coffins during the winter season."

In 1920 the City of Hamilton decided that another cemetery was needed, and voted to buy the old Carroll property along the northwest shore of the bay. Peter Carroll, a surveyor, settled on the property called Rock Bay (after Peter Rock, an earlier settler) in the 1840s. Staring across at Dundurn Castle must have given him ideas, so in the 1870s he built an impressive stone house, which he called Rock Bay. In 1908 the house was destroyed by fire. When the cemetery was being laid out, the last remains of the house were leveled. However, the gatehouse stood and was used as the entrance to the cemetery for years. Along with the Hamilton Cemetery, Woodland (for this was the name of the new cemetery) had some military connection to the War of 1812. On the bluff above Carroll's Point was the old gun pit, which had been used as a line of defence during the War of 1812. The workers had to remove it, in the process finding bayonets and other relics of the military occupation under the position of the old pit field pieces. Peter Carroll, whose property had become Woodland Cemetery, had died in 1876 and is therefore not buried there. His grave can be found on Burlington Heights, in the Hamilton Cemetery.

The outlying areas of Hamilton have literally dozens of cemeteries with names on the tombstones representing a veritable Who's Who of early settlement and development. Ancaster's St John's Anglican Church Cemetery, Dundas' Grove Cemetery, Stoney Creek's municipal cemetery and Glanbrook's White Church Cemetery are but a few of the dozens of sites that offer Hamiltonians a glimpse into the history of the people who came before us.

What is truly fascinating about cemeteries is that literally every tombstone tells a story. It represents a person or a family who lived and died and was buried in Hamilton. When exploring any of Hamilton's historic cemeteries one must always remember Marx Binkley's admonition:

"When this you see, oh think of me/Lest I should be forgotten."

WRITER BIOGRAPHIES

Roberta Bailey's family first came to the community in 1801. She was raised in Dundas and is proud to still call it home. She is a staff member of the Dundas Historical Society Museum.

Ronald Berenbaum attended Central Public School, Ryerson Senior Public School and Westdale Secondary School in Hamilton. He received a BA in history from Wilfrid Laurier University, and then spent 36 years as an investment broker in Hamilton. He is currently retired.

Bill Brigham was born in Hamilton and educated in Aldershot, Waterdown and Toronto. He has lived in the former Glanford Township since 1951. He spent four years in the RCAF, then worked for 33 years for Ontario Hydro in Hamilton and Middleport, retiring in 1983. Married with three children, he is part of the fifth generation of his family to attend St Paul's Glanford Anglican Church.

Janet Bertram Brown is the grandniece of Dr Tom Bertram and remembers him fondly. Early in the 1990s she took up researching the Bertram family tree, as started by her Uncle Graham Bertram, then president of the John Bertram and Sons Company of Dundas. In August 2000 she published the book *The Heritage of John Bertram. Growing with Canada 1850–2000*, a history of the Bertram family from the time John Bertram came to Canada in 1852 to the present. She is currently researching a book tracing the family back to 1066 AD and lives on the family farm in Brampton.

Marnie Burgess moved to Hamilton from Point Edward in 1988 to attend McMaster University. Pursuing her love of genealogy and local history, she now has a small business called Burgess Historical (www.burgesshistorical.com). Marnie does freelance historical researching for the public and for commercial businesses.

Stella Clark was born and raised in Hamilton. She works at Hamilton Public Library as a librarian assistant at the Stoney Creek branch, carrying out the children's programs, and is a member of the Stoney Creek Historical Society. As a member, Stella volunteers at the Erland Lee Museum, cataloguing artefacts and conducting tours. She and her husband, Paul, have two sons and two grandchildren.

Viola M. Collins is a charter member of the Beverly Heritage Society, and one of three members who produced an annual calendar of sketches of the area. She led a coalition group to re-establish and reopen the Westfield Heritage Village in 1990. She recently edited *Pioneers of Beverly — A Pictorial History*.

Clare Crozier is a member of the board of directors of the Dundas Historical Society Museum and the Cross-Melville Heritage District. Clare Crozier is the fourth generation of his family to live in Dundas. A lifelong interest in local history has led to his writing and lecturing on the town's early history.

Art French was born in Hamilton and raised in Mount Hope. He served in the RCAF and was an Air Canada pilot. Now retired, he lives on part of the farm settled by James French in 1838. Married with two children, he is a member of the Glanbrook Heritage Society and the Hamilton Local Architectural Conservation Advisory Committee (LACAC), and is president of the Hamilton-Wentworth Heritage Association.

Michael Gemmell was raised in Nepean, Ontario. He did an undergraduate degree in history and geography at Wilfrid Laurier University and a graduate degree in history at the University of Toronto. He worked between 1993 and 1998 in Kingston, Ontario, as a member of the Fort Henry Guard, before becoming curator of the Erland Lee Museum in Stoney Creek in 1998. An executive member of the Stoney Creek Historical Society, he lives in east Hamilton.

Carolyn Gray was an archivist for the Ontario Archives for 16 years. She is now with Publications Ontario. She is active with the Head-of-the-Lake Historical Society having served on the executive and on the publications committee. She has published extensively on Canadian and local history.

Paul Grimwood has been the Director of Music at Central Presbyterian Church, Hamilton, since 1979. He is a great-great-great grandson of Samuel Bamberger, who settled in Ancaster about 1806. He is the author of *Ancaster's Heritage, Volume 2*, which was published in 1998. He is the Chairman of the Ancaster Community Heritage Advisory Panel.

J. Brian Henley retired in 2001, after 28 years with the Hamilton Public Library. Brian continues to serve the Hamilton heritage community as a freelance writer and broadcaster. He is particularly interested in Hamilton's blend of natural and cultural history. Brian sits on the board of the Royal Botanical Gardens.

Margaret Houghton is the Special Collections Archivist at the Hamilton Public Library. A Hamiltonian born and bred, she has been employed by the library since 1978. She is a long-time member and president of the Players' Guild of Hamilton, and the president of the Head-of-the-Lake Historical Society. Margaret recently edited *Hamilton Street Names*.

Paul Kuzyk is vice-president of both the Head-of-the-Lake Historical Society and the Hamilton branch of the United Empire Loyalist Association. He is descended from the Horning family. Paul is also an avid researcher of railway history.

Stan Nowak is an active member of the Dundas Valley Historical Society. He is also involved with the Dundas Cactus Festival, the Dundas/Flamborough Environment Committee and the Hamilton-Wentworth Stewardship Council. Stan and his wife, Sally, have lived in Dundas since 1999.

Robert Rankin is a retired Hamilton police officer and amateur historian who works as a private investigator.

Donna Reid and **Robin McKee** are passionate about Hamilton history. Their young company, Historical Perspectives, is active with cemetery tours, photography, research and marketing.

Robin, a graduate of McMaster University and Mohawk College, has lived in Hamilton for 30 years. He is a member of the Hamilton Historical Board and recently was appointed vice-president of Community Heritage Ontario (CHO). Robin has worked at CH TV for 25 years and lives with his son, Spencer.

Donna grew up in Quebec City with history in her bloodstream. She attended Mount Allison University and Mount Royal College. For 20 years, she worked in marketing, sales and product promotion across Canada. She chose Hamilton as her home in 1998. Donna is an active volunteer with many heritage organizations and recently brought Doors Open to Hamilton.

Both Robin and Donna are members of Hamilton LACAC.

Shirley (Quance) Rumbles was born in Hamilton, but moved to Binbrook, to a farm at the corner of Sinclairville Road and Hall Road, in 1972. It was to Binbrook that her Quance ancestors emigrated from England in 1843. She is married with three children, and is secretary of the Glanbrook Heritage Society.

Spencer Snowling came to Hamilton to attend McMaster University in 1988, and completed his BEngMgt and PhD. He is now a Hamilton-area environmental engineer with Hydromantis Consulting Engineers. Spencer has a keen interest in local history, with an emphasis on historical engineering projects.

Carolyn Westoby was raised in Dundas and is proud to still call it home. She is a staff member of the Dundas Historical Society Museum.

Sylvia Wray was born in Hertfordshire, England, and received her schooling and college education there. She came to Canada in 1966 and taught at Hillfield Strathallan Colleges. In 1987 she returned to school, attending Mohawk College, where she took the Archives and Records Management course. Since 1990, she has operated the Flamborough Archives for the Waterdown-East Flamborough Heritage Society.

SELECT BIBLIOGRAPHY

Ambrose, Linda. *For Home & Country — The Centennial History of the Women's Institutes of Ontario.* Erin: Boston Mills Press, 1996.

Ancaster Township Historical Society. *Ancaster's heritage : a history of Ancaster Township.* Ancaster: Ancaster Township Historical Society, 1973.

Bailey, Thomas Melville, ed. *Wee Kirks and Stately Steeples: a history of the Presbytery of Hamilton: the Presbyterian Church in Canada 1800–1990.* Burlington: Eagle Press, 1990.

Bailey, Thomas Melville, ed.-in-chief (Volumes 1–4). *Dictionary of Hamilton Biography.* Hamilton: Dictionary of Hamilton Biography, 1981–1999.

Best, John C. *Thomas Baker McQuesten: Public Works, Politics and Imagination.* Hamilton: Corinth Press, ca 1991.

Binbrook Historical Society. *History and Heritage of Binbrook. 1792–1973.* Binbrook: Binbrook Historical Society, 1979.

Blaine, William E. *Ride Through the Garden of Canada: a short history of the Hamilton, Grimsby & Beamsville Electric Railway, 1894–1931.* 1967.

Campbell, Marjorie Freeman. *A Mountain and a City: the story of Hamilton.* Toronto: McClelland & Stewart, 1966.

Cooper, Charles. *Hamilton's Other Railway, 1853–2000: the Hamilton and Northwestern Railway in Retrospect.* Ottawa: Bytown Railway Society, ca 2001.

Dick-Lauder, Alma, et al. *Wentworth Landmarks.* Hamilton: Spectator Printing Co., 1897.

Dubro, James & Robin F. Rowland. *King of the Mob. Rocco Perri and the Women Who Ran His Rackets.* Markham: Penguin Books of Canada, 1987.

Dundas Heritage Association. *William Lyon Mackenzie Slept Here: Heritage Buildings of Dundas.* Produced by the Executive of the Dundas Heritage Association to mark Ontario's Bicentennial Year, 1984.

Dundas True Banner & Wentworth County Chronicle.

Elliott, James. *The Story of Billy Green and the Battle of Stoney Creek, June 6, 1813.* Stoney Creek: Stoney Creek Historical Society, ca 1994.

Erland Lee Museum archive files

Evans, Lois. *Hamilton, the story of a city.* Toronto: Ryerson Press, ca 1970.

Fisher, Rev. S.W. *Presbyterianism in West Flamboro' Church 1833–1908.* Dundas: Banner Printing Co., 1908.

Flamborough Archives archive files.

Globe & Mail, The.

Grimwood, Paul, ed. *Ancaster's heritage. Volume 2, A history of Ancaster Township.* Ancaster : Ancaster Township Historical Society, 1998.

Hamilton *Herald.*

Hamilton Spectator, The.

Hamilton *Times.*

Helson, Linda, ed. *Beyond Paradise, Building Dundas 1798–1850.* Dundas: The Local Architectural Conservation Advisory Committee of the Town of Dundas, 1996.

Hunt, C.E. *Whiskey and Ice. The Saga of Ben Kerr, Canada's Most Daring Rumrunner.* Toronto: Dundurn Press, 1995.

Jones, Andrew & Leonard Rutman. *In the children's Aid: J.J. Kelso and child welfare in Ontario.* Toronto: University of Toronto Press, 1981.

Johnston, Charles M. *The Head of the Lake: a history of Wentworth County*

Hamilton: Wentworth County Council, 1958.

———. *Loyalist Ancestors: Some Families of the Hamilton Area.* Toronto: Hamilton Branch United Empire Loyalist Association of Canada, 1986.

Miller, Floyd. *The Wild Children of the Urals.* New York: E.P. Dutton & Co., 1965.

Mills, Stanley. *Genealogical and Historical Records of the Mills and Gage Families. 1776–1926.* Hamilton: [S. Mills] 1926.

———. *Picturesque Dundas Revisited.* Dundas: Dundas Historical Society Museum, 1996.

———. *Saltfleet. Then and Now 1792–1973.* Fruitland: Corporation of the Town of Stoney Creek, 1973.

Smith, Llewellyn. *The House That Jam Built.* Markham: Baby Boomer Press, 1995.

Special Collections, Hamilton Public Library archive files.

West Flamborough Township Centennial. 1850–1950. Dundas: Star Printing co., 1950.

Woodhouse, T. Roy. *The History of the Town of Dundas (Volumes 1–3).* Dundas: Dundas Historical Society, 1965+.

Woods, Donald et al. *Waterdown & East Flamborough. 1867–1967.* Waterdown Centennial Committee, 1967.

INDEX